A Bit More Fry

Stephen Fry and Hugh Laurie are both writers, comedians, and actors. Stephen Fry wrote the script of the musical *Me and My Girl*. He regularly appears on television and radio and he writes a weekly column for the *Daily Telegraph*. Hugh Laurie starred in Ben Elton's play *Gasping* in the West End in 1990. Fry and Laurie both appeared regularly in *Blackadder* with Rowan Atkinson and they have starred in three series of *A Bit of Fry & Laurie*. They are currently working on a third series of *Jeeves and Wooster*.

Also available from Mandarin Paperbacks

A Bit of Fry & Laurie

STEPHEN FRY and HUGH LAURIE

A Bit More
Fry and Laurie

Mandarin

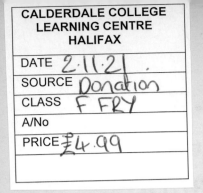
A Mandarin Paperback

A BIT MORE FRY AND LAURIE

First published in Great Britain 1991
by Mandarin Paperbacks
Michelin House, 81 Fulham Road, London SW3 6RB

Mandarin is an imprint of the Octopus Publishing Group,
a division of Reed International Books Ltd

Copyright © 1991 by Stephen Fry and Hugh Laurie

A CIP catalogue record for this title
is available from the British Library

ISBN 0 7493 1076 6

Stills from A BIT OF FRY AND LAURIE
copyright © 1991 BBC
Photograph of Stephen Fry and Hugh Laurie
copyright © 1990 by Mike Prior

Typeset by Falcon Typographic Art Ltd,
Edinburgh & London
Printed in Great Britain
by Cox & Wyman Ltd, Reading, Berkshire

Caution
All rights whatsoever in these sketches are strictly reserved
and applications for permission to perform them in whole or
in part must be made in advance, before rehearsals begin,
to David Higham Associates Ltd, 5–8 Lower John Street,
Golden Square, London W1R 4HA

To Bob Holness

*The authors would like to make public their
immense feelings of gratitude towards Roger
Ordish, Nick Symons and Jon Canter who
produced, produced and script-edited 'A Bit of
Fry & Laurie' Series 2 respectively. It would be
no exaggeration to say that their contributions
towards the programme were quite useful.*

S.F. & H.L.
St James's Club, Antigua
July 1991

Contents

Introduction

Stephen   Well, Hugh.

Hugh   Well, Stephen.

Stephen   Here we are again.

Hugh   More or less.

Stephen   More or less?

Hugh   Last time, if you remember, we were between MAPS and BIOGRAPHIES on the other side, but now they've changed the whole bookshop round.

Stephen   I think I prefer it here.

Hugh   Oh so do I.

Stephen   You get a nice view of the till and the fire exit, and we're only a short stroll away from the Leisure Interest section.

Hugh   I wouldn't want to go back, certainly.

Stephen   But anyway, Hugh, here we are again, with another collection of comedic ensketchments to thrill, tease and sexually arouse our reading public.

Hugh   More or less.

Stephen   More or less, yes. Wasn't it Big Ron Atkinson who said 'you can sexually arouse some of the people all of the time, and all of the people some of the time, but if you want to sexually arouse all of the people all of the time, you've got your work cut out to a certain extent'?

Hugh   No.

Stephen   Tsk. I'm thinking of Abba.

Hugh	Not wishing to interrupt or anything of that sort, but isn't it about time we rolled up our sleeves and got down to the job of introducing the ladies and gentlemen to this book?
Stephen	Haven't they met?
Hugh	Don't think so.
Stephen	I'm so sorry. I could have sworn they were both at the Hendersons' last New Year's Eve.
Hugh	What a night that was.
Stephen	Well, early evening.
Hugh	Yes. What an early evening that was.
Stephen	Well anyway, ladies and gentlemen, this is the book. Book, say hello to the ladies and gentlemen.
	Slight Pause.
Hugh	They seem to have hit it off remarkably well.
Stephen	Oh, I think it's going swimmingly.
Hugh	Well if you'll excuse me, I think I'll just nip to the lavatory.
Stephen	Hugh?
Hugh	Yes?
Stephen	We're in the lavatory.
Hugh	Of course we are. Tsk.
Stephen	You were thinking of Abba.
Hugh	Must have been.
Stephen	Hugh, my old china, I've a question for you.
Hugh	Off you go.
Stephen	Have I gone mad, or were we supposed to use this introduction as a way of issuing a warning?
Hugh	You've gone mad.

Stephen   If I have indeed gone mad, it's the sort of madness in which I have moments of achingly lucid sanity. Here's one now.

Hugh   Steady. Don't waste it.

Stephen   I seem to remember being given some advice by our solicitors.

Hugh   You're quite right. We were advised, by our solicitors, to write out a cheque to our solicitors.

Stephen   Made payable to bearer, if memory serves.

Hugh   Memory has served an ace in this instance, Stephen. We were asked to write out a cheque and advised that it was our duty to warn the potential purchaser of this book, this book with which they are already making such fast friends . . .

Stephen   Fast, but within the speed limit.

Hugh   Just.

Stephen   Just.

Hugh   It was our duty, I think I was saying . . .

Stephen   . . . before you were so attractively interrupted.

Hugh   . . . to warn the reader that these sketches are for external application only.

Stephen   On no account are they to be swallowed.

Hugh   Or performed in public without written permission from the publishers, unless and until you are the only human being left alive on the planet Earth.

Stephen   Which, in case you're starting to get alarmed, is an unlikely set of circumstances, and not one you would expect to come across every day of the week.

Hugh   But that's what you pay these legal johnnies for – covering angles that the rest of us wouldn't think of.

Stephen A humbling thought, Hugh. A humbling thought.

Hugh Any other duties we have to discharge, before the ladies and gentlemen ask this book back to their place for a cup of Horlicks and a snog?

Stephen Not really, except for heaven's sake make sure you've actually got some Horlicks.

Hugh Oh. That can be embarrassing, can't it?

Stephen Always have the wherewithal to back up your story. There's nothing worse than an idle boast.

Hugh Wasn't it the Swedish pop group Abba who said 'a man who claims to have Horlicks when he hasn't, is no man at all – and certainly wouldn't be welcome at Sheffield Wednesday'?

Stephen No.

Hugh Oh.

Stephen It was G.K. Chesterton.

Hugh B'bye.

Stephen B'bye.

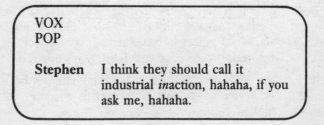

VOX
POP

Stephen I think they should call it industrial *in*action, hahaha, if you ask me, hahaha.

Dammit 1

Stephen and Hugh are pacing the boardroom.

Stephen   Dammit Peter.

Hugh   John?

Stephen   Dammit four times round the car park and back in for another dammit.

Hugh   Do I get the feeling that something's on your mind, John?

Stephen   Come on, Peter, you know what the hell I'm talking about.

Hugh   At a guess I'd say that this had something to do with the DDL Enterprises takeover bid?

Stephen   You know it's funny, Peter. Four years. Four hard years I've put into building up this Health Club. And now I'm supposed to stand by and let a bunch of wet-arsed college kids take it all away from me.

Hugh   I know, John.

Stephen   If only Marjorie hadn't left us the way she did . . .

Hugh   Marjorie? Hell John, you can't go blaming yourself for that. You and Marjorie had . . .

Stephen   Had what, Peter? A marriage that was nothing more than a bad joke, and not even a very good one?

Hugh   You made some mistakes, John, that's all. You and Marjorie had different ideas about where the company was headed. End of story.

Stephen   But dammit, Marjorie was good, Peter.

Hugh	A good wife, or a good business partner?
Stephen	Is there a difference, Peter?
Hugh	I hope so, John.
Stephen	And now, while we're up to our arses in a major takeover scrap, she's sunning herself in the South of France.
Hugh	South of Wales actually, John.
Stephen	Well, wherever the blue-rinsed hell she is. Oh what a damned fool I've been.
Hugh	John, listen to me, this is no time for you to start feeling sorry for yourself.
Stephen	But dammit all sideways, Peter . . .
Hugh	John. Do something for me. Take a look out of this window.
Stephen	What is this, Peter? Some sort of game?
Hugh	No game, John. Look out there and tell me what you see.
Stephen	I see a car park.
Hugh	Well that's funny, John. Because the last time you looked out of that window, you saw an idea. Don't you remember?
Stephen	Yes. I remember.
Hugh	I thought so.
Stephen	I remember thinking that that would be the best place for the car park.
Hugh	Dammit John, I'm talking about the big idea. The dream that you and I shared. The dream of a health club that would put Uttoxeter on the goddamned map once and for all.
Stephen	Yeah, well maybe . . .

Hugh	Maybe? Maybe? I don't believe I'm hearing this. What the hell's happened to the old John?
Stephen	We pulled it down when we built the car park.
Hugh	Dammit John, you're not hearing me.
Stephen	Peter I . . .
Hugh	Don't Peter I me! We've got *that* close. And you're going to lie down and just walk away.
Stephen	Peter, don't hassle me. I'm tired.
Hugh	Tired be damned!
Stephen	A man's got to know when he's licked, Peter. And I know the feeling. I've been licked before.
Hugh	The Lord's Saints preserve us.
Stephen	Did I ever tell you about the time Marjorie licked me? Licked me good and proper? Well I've got the same feeling now, Peter, and it's sore. Maybe it's time to move on.
Hugh	John. I'm going to tell you what I see out of this window.
Stephen	Is this another one of your games, Peter?
Hugh	Same game, John. Different rules. *(Looking out)* I see Tom and Sally and Debbie . . .
Stephen	I thought Sally was off with the flu . . .
Hugh	Exactly, John! Exactly! But she's come in today because she believes in you! God knows why! She believes in what you're trying to do here in Uttoxeter. And you're going to just turn your back on those kids? You're going to walk away from . . . dammit, I make no apology, a vision?
Stephen	Dammit Peter, maybe you're right.
Hugh	You're damn right maybe I'm right.

7

Stephen	Damn, double damn, and an extra pint of damn for the weekend.
Hugh	Daaaaamn!
Stephen	Right, Peter.
Hugh	Damn?
Stephen	Get a fax over to Cliff at Harlinson's. Extraordinary General Meeting, 3.00p.m. today. Call Janet, and see if we can pull Martin in from . . . where the hell is Martin?
Hugh	High Wycombe.
Stephen	And get Sarah in here. We've got an agenda to work up.
Hugh	Welcome back to the fight, John. Sorry if I was a little rough on you back there.
Stephen	Hell, Peter, I deserved it. I was a damned fool.
Hugh	And if Marjorie calls . . . ?
Stephen	If Marjorie calls . . . *(Pause)* Tell her I'm busy.
Both	DAAAAAAMN!!!

VOX
POP

Hugh	Moira Stewart . . . and Jill Gascoigne . . . neither of them wrote back. Can you believe these people? I mean how much trouble can it be to just bung a pair of stockings in the post?

Dinner With Digby

Kensington dinner party set. Candles, tablecloth, fruit, epergne etc. At the head of the table, dinner-jacketed, is Susan Digby, played by Stephen. Hugh, similarly DJ-ed, plays Jeremy James Duff, a poncy John Julius Norwich type, there is also Leslie Crith of the Independent.

Camera is on Stephen, who is talking, but studio sound isn't up yet.

Captions   Susan Digby with dinner guests

Camera pans along the table to Hugh, lips also moving wordlessly.

Jeremy James Duff, travel-writer, broadcaster and journalist

Pan/track along to Leslie.

Leslie Crith, the *Independent*.

Stephen   . . . and similarly louche places. But Jeremy, I must tell you. I was in Venice last year.

Hugh   Ah, *la serenissima*!

Stephen   That's right. You probably know more than anyone else in the world about Venice.

Hugh   The Queen of the Adriatic.

Stephen   Is only one of the things you've been called. I was walking across the Rialto, returning from a walk that took in Santa Maria della Salute and San Giorgio Romano . . .

Leslie   Along the Giudecca?

Stephen	Along the Giudecca, and I think I'm right in saying that I counted no less that seventy-nine backpackers ...
Leslie	Backpackers, oh dear lord.
Stephen	... who were 'doing', as I believe they say, the Accademia.
Hugh	Ugh, ugh, ugh, ugh. Tourists, you see.
Stephen	And I remember thinking, they're taking away our Venice.
Hugh	Our Venice is being taken away from us. It's crawling with Germans.
Leslie	And Italians.
Stephen	Our Venice is sinking under their weight, not just physically, but the beauty, Jeremy, the grandeur of our Venice is sinking under the blue nylon of their wind-cheaters, their Cola-Coca cans, their eternal flashlight photo-cameras.
Leslie	And that monstrous tinny noise that emanates from their Sony Walkmans.

Hugh and Stephen are baffled.

Stephen	Their ... ?
Hugh	Erm?
Stephen	Oh you mean those personal stereophonic discothèques?
Hugh	Stop it, stop it, stop it at once.
Stephen	If only ...
Hugh	Ah, yes well now you see, I have campaigned for years now to have tourists banned from Venice.
Stephen	Have you? Have you?
Hugh	I have, I have. It sounds very harsh, very cruel, very ...

Stephen	Déglanté?
Hugh	Very déglanté, thank you. But I'm sure it's the only way.
Stephen	Ng, ng, ng, ng.
Leslie	Who was it, who was it, who said '*He* is a tourist, *you* are a holidaymaker but *I* am a traveller?'
Hugh	Oh, was it Humbert Wolfe?
Stephen	It was Cocteau, surely?
Hugh	It doesn't sound very Cocteau.
Stephen	But then Cocteau never did, which is how you can always tell it's Cocteau.
Hugh	True, true. Trouché!
Leslie	Of course it's not just Venice is it?
Hugh	It's not just Venezia, Venedig, Veneeess, not by a very long stroke.
Leslie	Our whole world is being stained.
Stephen/Hugh	Stained, stained.
Stephen	Eheu fugaces! O tempora, o mores, Jeremy.
Hugh	Yes indeed.
Leslie	I blame television. I'm sorry but I do.
Hugh	(*Pained at the thought*) Ah . . . ah, ah, television. That fearful Mervyn Bragg.
Stephen	Mervyn Bragg, stop it, don't, shush, now please, really. If I had my way with Mervyn Bragg . . .
Hugh	No one would be in the least surprised.
	Lots of laughter.
Leslie	This is most awfully good Tarte Citron.

11

Stephen/Hugh

Er . . . ?

Leslie   Tarte Citron.

Stephen   Oh, the lemon pie. Thank you. I always say I could never really be friends with someone who didn't love lemon pie.

Hugh   Susan, don't be sly, did you make it yourself?

Stephen   Let's just say I made it to the shops in time to buy it.

Hugh/Leslie

Marks & Spencer?

Stephen   Who else, but M & S?

Hugh   M & S!

Leslie   M & S! M et S. They are simply amazing aren't they?

Hugh   And have you tried their new boxer shorts?

Stephen   No I haven't, I haven't, I haven't.

Leslie   I have. Delicious.

Hugh   And their dips! Oh bless me, their dips.

Leslie   In my local one there's a really marvellous school.

Stephen   A primary school?

Leslie   Oh yes. Both mine and my husband's children go there.

Stephen   Mine's just opened a hospital section.

Hugh   Have they? Have they really?

Stephen   Oh yes, you can go in and have minor operations, everything.

Hugh   In the one just round the corner from me they sell weaponry.

Stephen   Is that right?

12

Hugh	Oh it is. Quite right.
Leslie	Mine too.
Hugh	I bought an F1-11 there last week . . . so *fresh* . . . I swear it was made that day . . .
	Fading out.
Stephen	And of course if you're unhappy, you can always go back and change it . . .

VOX
POP

Hugh   *(Holding up plate)* See this? You could eat your dinner off this.

13

Commentators

*Hugh and Stephen are two rather doddery old
commentators.*

Stephen   As we look down now, on this glorious July
afternoon . . . what a splendid sight it is, Peter.

Hugh   It's an absolute picture, isn't it? The sun beating
down . . .

Stephen   Beautiful day . . .

Hugh   The crowds . . . not a seat to be had anywhere . . .

Stephen   Packed house . . .

Hugh   Absolutely packed . . . and the grass looking so
lovely . . .

Stephen   Green as anything.

Hugh   Green as you like. Absolutely as green as
could be . . .

Stephen   Grass has never looked greener . . . The
groundsman Arthur . . .

Hugh   Alan.

Stephen   Is it? Alan Dixon. Alan Dixon has done a
marvellous job . . .

Hugh   Marvellous job, he really has. What a scene.

Stephen   Marvellous scene . . .

Hugh   Oh I say there's a bus.

Stephen   Yes, look there's a beautiful old English . . . what
is that? Number 29?

Hugh	It's a 29 bus, yes.
Stephen	A beautiful English 29 bus, yes, what a marvellous scene. Grass, sun, bus, marvellous.
Hugh	Yes, that bus making its way now along the Garboldisham road.
Stephen	Garboldisham, beautiful village that is . . .
Hugh	Absolutely delightful village . . .
Stephen	Garboldisham. What a lovely name.
Hugh	Lovely name. Lovely English name.
Stephen	Hello, there are some people getting off the bus . . .
Hugh	Look out . . .
Stephen	They're off to enjoy their good old English strawberries and cream . . .
Hugh	Oh English, yes, watch out for those German strawberries . . .
Stephen	Not the same . . .
Hugh	Not the same thing at all . . . English strawberries and cream . . . 29 bus going down the Garboldisham road . . .
Stephen	Grass . . .
Hugh	Cream . . .

They begin to gather momentum in some sort of unpleasant sexual exchange of fruity things.

Stephen	Garboldisham . . .
Hugh	Crowds . . .
Stephen	The South Downs . . .
Hugh	Malvern hills rolling like a . . .
Stephen	Motor cars . . . leather gloves . . .

Hugh	A quarter pound of Mrs Faversham's extra strong peppermints . . .
Stephen	Ovaltine . . .
Hugh	Wellington boots . . .
Stephen	Cream . . .
Hugh	Heaps of cream . . . cream and lawnmowers . . .
Stephen	Summer holidays in Cromer . . .
Hugh	Vaulting over a stile in a country lane . . .
Stephen	Catching sticklebacks in an old tin can . . .
Hugh	'Honestly nanny, I never touched them . . .'
Stephen	Piano lessons with Mrs Duckworth . . .
Hugh	Father's hands on the steering wheel . . .
Stephen	Sit up straight!
Hugh	Going faster and faster . . .
Stephen	Locked in the cupboard for being rude to Mrs Howlett . . .
Hugh	Take the Wolseley for a run . . .
Stephen	England . . . Elgar . . . Malvern Hills.
Hugh	Bath Olivers. Play the game . . . elbows off the table.
Stephen	Who's a brave soldier then? Nanny's hands all steamy and starched.
Hugh	England! England and cream . . .
Stephen	Custard cream . . .
Hugh	Strawberries and cream . . .
Stephen	Strawberries and English cream . . .

16

Hugh   Take the B road to Petersfield. England.

(Shouting now)

Stephen   Creamy England!

Hugh   England!

Stephen   Cream!

Hugh   The roast cream of old England.

Stephen   Oh.

Hugh   Oh I say.

A post-coital interlude.

Stephen   And here comes Nigel Lawson now . . .

VOX
POP

Stephen   A challenge for her? Yes I've got
a challenge for her. Why doesn't
she see if she can bleeding well
BLEEP herself. For charity
obviously.

First Kiss

Hugh   My first kiss. I suppose everyone can remember their first kiss. Nothing quite lives up to it, does it? I was eleven years old I remember and my great-uncle had come to stay for a few weeks on parole. We used to play a game where I would sit on his lap and he would pretend to be a train. Then one day . . .

Stephen comes on.

Stephen   Hugh, Hugh, what are you saying?

Hugh   I was telling the ladies and gentlemen about my first kiss.

Stephen   Yes, but Hugh, this is a delicate area, I really don't think –

Hugh   We agreed that 'A Bit More Fry & Laurie' was going to be an arena for the expression of all kinds of ideas and experiences that wouldn't normally find their way on to television, didn't we?

Stephen   We did, we did agree.

Hugh   So my surprise at feeling a tongue suddenly . . .

Stephen   Hugh, there are valid arenas and valid arenas. This is not one of them.

Hugh   But I want that experience to be understood, it may help others to know that they're not the first to feel that wet . . .

Stephen   Hugh. Believe me this is a whole can of worms you're opening here, and if there is one single taboo left, one unmentionable subject not fit for comic treatment, you've just mentioned it.

Hugh   But surely there's nothing so very odd about it. There I was, on my great-uncle's lap and in came Lucy.

Stephen   Lucy.

Hugh   Yes, Lucy.

Stephen   And how old was Lucy?

Hugh   Oh, twelve I think. And I kissed her.

Stephen   You kissed her.

Hugh   Yes.

Stephen   You've done this deliberately haven't you?

Hugh   Done what?

Stephen   You set it up to make it sound as if –

Hugh   As if what?

Stephen   Never mind. Get on with it.

Hugh   All right. So I kissed Lucy, and was very surprised to feel her tongue pop out. It was my first real snog and I loved it. You can imagine that I fell in love instantly. Sadly the next year Lucy developed distemper and had to be put down.

Stephen   Doh.

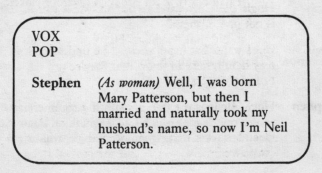

VOX
POP

Stephen   *(As woman)* Well, I was born Mary Patterson, but then I married and naturally took my husband's name, so now I'm Neil Patterson.

Brainstorm

Five people around a table: flimsies, photographs, graphics etc. The people are Stephen, a copy-writer, Hugh a ditto, Fee, an imponderably stupid graphic artist, Rhiannon an aggressive producer, and Dick, another copy-writer.

Stephen   *(Standing and stretching)* All right. Before we crack off on this new campaign, I'd like you all to get to know each other. Rhiannon, you must all know, worked on that draught-excluder commercial, the one with the young guy in the American leather jacket, driving around in an old pink Cadillac.

Rhiannon   Hi, everyone.

Hugh   Hiya. That was a great television commercial. Made me weep.

Rhiannon   Thanks.

Fee   That was really beautiful work actually. Because I saw it.

Stephen   Fee of course was the power behind that brilliant campaign for Total Protein Concept Balance System shampoo, the one with . . . how did it go? It had a guy in an American leather jacket, driving round in a . . .?

Fee   . . . an old pink Cadillac. Hi.

Rhiannon   That was bitchingly good.

Hugh   World class, world class.

Stephen   Jake, obviously, came up with the commercial for Dong Jeans, which had a guy in an American leather jacket driving round in a . . . what was it, Jake?

20

Hugh	It was an old blue Cadillac.
Rhiannon	Incredible.
Fee	Genius.
Stephen	I hardly need say that Jake's ideas tend to be a little bit off the wall.
Hugh	Yeah, I'm crazy.
Stephen	And joining us from an out of town agency is Dick. Dick's just come from working on that fabulous commercial for 'Pretension' by Calvin Klein ...
Dick	Er ... no ... that wasn't me.
Stephen	Oh ... they've sent us another Dick, have they? Well what was the last thing you worked on, Dick?
Dick	I wrote an advertisement for Tideyman's Carpets.
Stephen	Yeah?
Dick	It had a picture of lots of carpets, and a voice said 'Tideyman's Carpets, sale now on'.
	Slightly embarrassed silence.
Stephen	Great stuff.
Hugh	Yeah, fantastic.
Stephen	So we have a team here with one hell of a proven track record. Drinks anyone?
Hugh	Jack Daniels.
Rhiannon	Jack Daniels suits me.
Stephen	Bourbons for everyone then, yeah?
Dick	A Fanta for me, please.
	Stephen is at the fridge.
Stephen	OK. Floor's yours, Jake.

Hugh rises; he's a gum-chewing cockney whizz.

Hugh   What we've got here, people, is a big campaign for a new bank account. The Nexus Bank Account.

Stephen   I want to stress new here. New means different. That means *different* advertising.

Fee   Different.

Hugh   Different.

Stephen   Different.

Rhiannon I want it on record that I think this should be different.

Stephen   Point taken.

Fee   Can I butt in here?

Stephen   Sure, Fee.

Fee   Thanks.

Stephen   All right. So let's brainstorm it. Let's find a hook, a peg, an angle, a line, a channel . . . what is it that's going to *sell* this bank account?

Rhiannon What's going to sell that guts and kidneys out of it?

They all start clicking their fingers, clapping their hands. All except Dick that is, who sits there slightly surprised by their behaviour.

Hugh   Right well. How about . . . how about . . . a guy.

Rhiannon Young?

Hugh   A young guy, thanks darling, he's wearing . . . I dunno . . . what?

Fee   Sweatshirt?

Rhiannon Jeans?

Dick   A cardigan?

22

Hugh	No wait . . . What about an American leather jacket?
	They whoop and emote.
Stephen	An American leather jacket!
Rhiannon	Jake I hate you!
Fee	That's brilliant. That's really brilliant because people wear those.
Dick	Um . . .
Stephen	Yes, Dick?
Dick	It's not very different.
	Silence.
Stephen	Maybe Dick's right.
Hugh	Hell I'm not married to the idea.
Fee	It always worried me, I must say.
Rhiannon	I always hated the bastard.
Stephen	OK. Clean slate, everybody. Let's start afresh from scratch one.
Hugh	What about a Canadian leather jacket . . .
Stephen	Suede . . .
Rhiannon	That's it! A Canadian suede leather jacket. And . . . *(She's got an idea coming)* and . . .
Hugh	Yeah?
Rhiannon	*(It dawns on her)* HE'S DRIVING AN OLD CAR!!!!
Fee	An *old* car! He's driving an *old* car!
Hugh	An old Jaguar!
Stephen	What about *(Thumps the table)* a Cadillac. He's driving a sodding old pink Cadillac!

Thunderous applause and cheering.

Rhiannon   Something.

Stephen   Perfect. Amazing work. Right, well. Lunch everyone?

They make as if to go.

Dick   That's it, is it?

Hugh   I see what Dick's getting at. We need something else as well.

Stephen   Okay, let's run with Dick's something else as well idea for the moment. The young guy has got to have something else as well.

People start getting up and looking at things.

Hugh   *(Picking up a coffee cup)* Something aspirational . . . Coffee . . .?

Stephen   Bigger!

Rhiannon   *(Picking up a stapler)* A stapler?

Stephen   Bigger than that!

Fee   A telephone? They can be quite big. I've seen.

Stephen   Much bigger!!

Hugh   Wait a minute . . .

Stephen   Jake's got something . . .

Rhiannon   What have you got, Jake?

Hugh   A baby. The guy's got a baby.

Stephen   New man, caring, tender, Jake I love you!

Fee   That's brilliant because people have those. A really huge baby.

Rhiannon   A really huge American baby.

Stephen   Wearing . . .?

24

All	An American leather jacket!!!
Stephen	So what are we saying? What are we saying about Nexus here? We're saying . . .
Hugh	We're saying 'this bank account is so good it will virtually make you American'.
Dick	Why are we saying that?
Hugh	Well, um . . . we're saying that . . . we're saying that because . . . we're saying that . . . Problem, Dick? Objection?
Dick	Well why does everything have to be American? Why couldn't it be an English leather jacket?
Hugh	Oh dear.
Stephen	Dick, I'm sensing you're not with us on this. You have another idea?
Dick	Well, I have worked something out as a matter of fact.
Fee	We're all ears.
Rhiannon	We are. Nothing but ears.
Stephen	I'm just one huge ear, Dick.
Dick	Um . . . *(Reading)* 'The Nexus bank Account. It offers the same rate of interest as every other young person's account and comes with a perfectly normal plastic card. You may find it quite useful.'

Stephen grabs Dick's notepad.

Stephen	Dick, Dick, Dick.

Stephen hands notepad to Hugh.

The anti-ad. Dick, you've got something there.

Hugh	Christ, I'm beginning to see what you mean! 'The Nexus Bank Account. It's not so bad really.'

Rhiannon	Sen-Christing-sational.
Fee	You're so clever, Dick. Because that's a really good idea.
Hugh	You've cracked it, Dick.
Rhiannon	Dick's cracked the son of a bastard.
Stephen	Dick's cracked it!!
Fee	Dick, you're a star.
Dick	Well, looks like the Fantas are on me then.

VOX
POP

Stephen *(Showing the places on his body)* They cut me right round that way to see if they could find anything. Then they had a dig about down here. Still nothing. So they poked this thing up my . . . you know . . . had a look up there. Nothing. I'm going through the red channel next time.

Spies/Pigeons

Hugh knocks and enters the spies' office. It is empty, but the window is open.

Hugh   Morning Control, I was just. . . . oh.

He looks round the office, disappointed. He is about to leave when the phone on Control's desk starts ringing; Hugh is unsure about answering it, but eventually does.

Hello, this is the Secret Service. . . . No, I'm afraid Control's not here at the moment, who is this please? Oh hello Mrs Control . . . No it's rather strange. I just popped into Control's office to see if he'd like a cup of coffee, because it's nearly eleven o'clock, and there's no one here . . . I can't think where he can have got to. I agree with you, Mrs Control, that he'll probably turn up. Bye bye.

He hangs up, just as Stephen enters.

Stephen   Hello Tony.

Hugh   Control, there you are. I was beginning to worry.

Stephen   Oh?

Hugh   Mrs Control has just been on the telephone, and between me and Mrs Control, neither of us seemed to know where you were.

Stephen   Ah. Well let me explain, Tony. But let me first ask whether you notice anything unusual about the office?

Hugh   Let's see. The only thing that struck me about it was that you weren't in it, Control. Apart from that . . .

27

Stephen	What about the window, Tony?
Hugh	The window, of course! The window always used to be slightly further to the left!
Stephen	Not quite, Tony.
Hugh	Oh. It was a bit of a guess, actually.
Stephen	No, the window is in the same place that it's always been. I know we talked about moving it, and you very kindly looked into the feasibility of the whole thing, but after a while I had to make the difficult decision that that particular game just wasn't worth the candle.
Hugh	Yes, and after you'd made that decision, I remember you talked at some length about what you saw as the loneliness of command.
Stephen	That's right, Tony. No, what's unusual about the window is that it's open.
Hugh	You're right, Control. Is this in some way connected to your not having been in the office earlier on?
Stephen	Yes, Tony, it is. You see, I fell out of the window.
Hugh	Control, I can only say how sorry I am, and ask whether you were hurt in any way.
Stephen	To my surprise, Tony, I am in fact not hurt at all.
Hugh	Well that is something of a blessing anyway.
Stephen	Yes, you're right.
Hugh	Because one of the other things about being Control, I've always thought, is that your office is on the sixth floor, so that in the event of something like this happening, you have got slightly further to fall than if you were in the Record department which is located on the first floor of this building.

Stephen   Very similar thoughts were going through my mind, Tony, as I travelled towards the pavement with gathering speed.

Hugh   But how did this whole sorry business come about, Control?

Stephen   Tony, I've a confession to make. One of the things I like to do before you very kindly bring me my morning coffee is feed the pigeons who perch on my window sill.

Hugh   Control, I can't say I'm surprised. There had been some rumour in the canteen to that effect.

Stephen   Well then, I'm glad to be able to silence those wagging tongues one way or another. I do feed the pigeons, and it was while I was doing this that I fell out of the window.

Hugh   Control, I think I can picture the scene. There you were, at the open window, so engrossed in what you were doing that you neglected not to fall out of the window. Am I fairly near the mark?

Stephen   Spot on, Tony.

Hugh   I thought so. And I'll tell you another thing that has resulted from this whole adventure.

Stephen   What's that?

Hugh   It's after 11 o'clock and you've not had your coffee.

Stephen   You're right. Huh. It never rains but it pours, eh Tony?

Hugh   Yes, Control, but quite often it rains and pours at the same time.

Stephen   Yes. Well on your way to the coffee-making area, could you ask Valerie to pop out and apologise to an old lady who was selling flowers outside the main entrance.

Hugh	I'll certainly do that, Control. Did she happen to be the unlucky one who broke your fall?
Stephen	No. She was fortunate in that respect, Tony. But she might be a little upset that her young grandson did.
Hugh	Fair enough, Control. Tell you what then. She might welcome a cup of coffee too!
Stephen	Good thinking, Tony. B-bye!
Hugh	B-bye.

VOX
POP

Hugh   Both of them. Stark naked and
at it like knives. BBC 1 at seven
o'clock in the evening. It was
disgusting. I don't know what
that David Attenborough thinks
he's about.

Society

A sitting room. A doorbell rings. A woman gets up and answers the door to Stephen and Hugh. Most of the way through Hugh is repeating everything Stephen says, a fraction of a second later.

Stephen Morning.

Hugh Morning.

Stephen We're from the Westminster Society . . .

Hugh Society . . .

Stephen We wondered if we could come in and talk to you about our aims, and the possibility of you joining us.

Hugh . . . joining us, possibly, who knows?

Woman Well . . .

Stephen Thank you . . .

Hugh So much.

Stephen I'm Mr Willis. And this is Mr Barraclough.

Hugh Barraclough . . .

Stephen No relation, in case you're wondering.

Woman Sorry?

Stephen We're not related to each other, in case you thought we were.

Woman Well why should you be?

Stephen Well we shouldn't, that's what I'm saying. We shouldn't be related and we're not. Hence the totally different names.

31

Woman	So, what can I do for you?
Stephen	As I say, my colleague and I are thinking of founding this society . . .
Hugh	Society . . .
Stephen	Would you be interested in joining us?
Hugh	. . . perhaps joining us?
Woman	And what is this society for?
Stephen	It's . . .
Hugh	Well . . .

They look at each other.

Stephen	Well obviously this is one of the things we need to look at . . .
Hugh	Look at it very carefully indeed . . .
Stephen	And I think you've already shown that you would be a very useful member . . .
Hugh	Useful member of the society.
Woman	But you said you had some aims.
Stephen	I don't think we did.
Hugh	. . . did say that, we may have done . . .
Woman	But when I answered the door, you said could you come in and talk about the aims of your society.

They look uncomfortable.

Stephen	Well that's a matter of opinion . . .
Hugh	Subjective opinion, really . . .
Woman	Well all right, but what is the point of this society? I mean you've got to have a point, otherwise . . . there's no point.
Stephen	Hmm. That's a good point.

Hugh	Well made . . .
Woman	I mean are you going to collect postage stamps?
Stephen	Yes.
Hugh	Definitely. Collect postage stamps.
Woman	Or are you going to practise Highland dancing?
Stephen	Yes. Stamps and Highland dancing are very high on the society's agenda.
Hugh	Hardly anything higher on the agenda than those two.
Woman	Or talk about Roman ruins in Shropshire?
Stephen	Definitely that.
Hugh	That's even higher on the agenda. That's right up at the top.
Woman	But you don't know?
Stephen	Know what?
Hugh	Know what, precisely?
Woman	You don't know for certain what the society is going to be for?
Stephen	Well, we have made one or two notes . . .
Hugh	Just one or two . . .
Woman	Yes?
Stephen	But unfortunately, not to do with the society.
Hugh	On a completely separate matter.
Stephen	However, to answer your question in the spirit in which it was asked . . .
Hugh	In that very selfsame spirit . . .
Stephen	My view is that the society should be run in the interests of its members.

Hugh	Brilliant. That's my view too. Members.
Stephen	But you see, until we have some members, we don't really have any interests.
Hugh	You might say that our hands are tied ...
Stephen	So. Will you help us?
Woman	Can I make a suggestion?
Stephen	Of course. Suggestions.
Hugh	Eureka. Suggestions.
Stephen	Tuesdays and Thursdays could be suggestion evenings.
Woman	No, can I make a suggestion now. And that is that you come back when you've decided what this society is supposed to be for. I can't stand here talking all day.
Stephen	Now there's an idea.
Hugh	Definitely an idea there.
Stephen	A society for people who can't stand here talking all day.
Hugh	All day and all night.
Stephen	I think that would be a very popular society. ...
Hugh	Flock to join that society ...
Stephen	When you think of all the people who knock on your door.
Hugh	Knock on your bell ...
Stephen	Jehovah's witnesses ...
Hugh	Witnesses to the Jehovah's incident ...
Stephen	Charity collectors ... estate agents ... small boys wanting their ball back ...

34

Hugh	The ball which accidentally went over the fence back . . .
Stephen	Could we interest you in joining that society?
Woman	I'm going to shut the door now.
Stephen	Excellent.
Woman	What?
Stephen	Shutting the door indicates a definite interest in joining a society for people who can't stand here talking all day . . .
Hugh	Total commitment to the society.

She slams the door. Cut to a shot of them outside the door.

Stephen	Well that's one member for our society, then . . .
Hugh	One member for definite member . . .
Stephen	Shall we try next door?
Hugh	Next door, why not?

VOX
POP

Stephen	He just picked me up and slapped me. Really hard. I cried and cried, but he wouldn't take any notice. Then he put a plastic tag round my wrist, cut my umbilical cord and put me in a cot. It was awful.

Introducing My Grandfather To . . .

Hugh in studio with an old man and Stephen.

Hugh   Hello and welcome to 'Introducing My Grandfather To'. Tonight I shall be Introducing My Grandfather To the novelist and corporate accountant Sir Benton Asher. Good evening Sir Benton.

Stephen   Good evening.

Hugh   May I introduce you to my grandfather? Grandfather, this is Sir Benton Asher.

Stephen   *(Shaking hands with old man)* How do you do?

Old Man   Yes.

Hugh   Next week I shall be introducing my grandfather to Desmond Lynham. Until then, goodnight.

VOX POP

Hugh   Everyone looks on me as the local historian. But it's amazing what a fascinating history Solihull does in fact have. But the odd thing is that I am the only person, so far as I know, to find it even remotely interesting.

Combat Games

Stephen rings the doorbell of a semi, dressed in an anorak and sensible hat. The door swings open, but there is no one there. Stephen enters hesitantly.

Stephen   Hello? Hello? Yoo hoo? Anyone at ho ...

Hugh springs out, hanging upside down, dressed in camouflage gear with a headband and khaki greasepaint all over his face: he is holding a gun.

Oh good afternoon.

Hugh   In a combat situation you would be dead meat, mister.

Stephen   Sorry?

Hugh   If you'd have been some sort of gook, I would have burned you away and had your arse for breakfast.

Stephen   Oh. Right.

Hugh   You're not a gook, though, are you?

Stephen   I hope not.

Hugh   No. Gooks don't wear anoraks, as far as I can ascertain. Pass friend.

Stephen   Thank you. Are you anything to do with Martin Wilson's Recreational Wargames Limited?

Hugh   Indeed. I am he.

Stephen   Who?

Hugh   I am Colonel 'Mad' Martin Wilson, and Recreational Wargames are very much my business.

Stephen	Oh good. I'm interested in taking part in one of these combat games.
Hugh	Well, you've come to the right place. This is what I call the game zone.
Stephen	I see. This is where the combat games take place, is it?
Hugh	That is correct, my friend. Trust no one and nothing. The game zone is full of surprises.
Stephen	Yes. The first surprise is, it's your front room.
Hugh	A front room equipped for war. This, for example, is an anti-personnel magazine rack.
Stephen	Is it?
Hugh	No. But you couldn't possibly have known that.
Stephen	Is this what we're going to play with?
Hugh	Please do not aim your weapon unless you intend to discharge it, and then only if in a full combat situation.
Stephen	It's a water pistol.
Hugh	Yes. Loaded with live water.
Stephen	Righty ho.
Hugh	I will count to ten, and you will secrete yourself somewhere in the game zone, preferably in a potential ambush position. I will then come after you in what I choose to call a search and destroy mission.
Stephen	Crikey.
Hugh	And remember, the first rule of the game zone is, there are no rules. And the second rule is, don't go into the kitchen. It's out of bounds.
Stephen	Understood.
Hugh	Right, the game time begins . . .

38

A woman enters from the kitchen.

Woman   Do you want some tea, Martin? Oh good afternoon.

Stephen   Hello.

Woman   I was just making some tea for my husband. Would you fancy a cup?

Stephen   Oh that'd be very nice. Thank you.

Woman   Won't be a minute.

She goes back into the kitchen.

Stephen   That's very kind of her.

Hugh   Coo. You really are dead meat. Never trust civilians.

Stephen   But she's your wife, isn't she?

Hugh   She said she was my wife. But she could easily be a gook, for all you know.

Stephen   Well surely gooks don't wear aprons, do they?

Hugh   Never mind.

Stephen   Cooks do.

Hugh   All right. Game time begins. One. Two. Three. Four . . .

Stephen tiptoes out of the room.

Five. Six. Seven. Eight, nine, ten seconds of game time have elapsed.

Hugh opens his eyes and looks round the room: then he suddenly drops on to the floor and starts to move around the room in a series of somersaults and ridiculous combat poses. Eventually he is forced to give up.

(*Calling out*) Right. Congratulations, my friend. You are the first person ever to have outwitted Colonel

'Mad' Martin Wilson in a game situation. Hello?
Tscch. Honestly. That chap is dead meat.

Mrs Wilson enters with a tray of tea things.

Woman	There you are dear.
Hugh	Thank you dear.
Woman	Where's your friend?
Hugh	Friend? He is the enemy, dear.
Woman	Well doesn't he want his tea, then?
Hugh	Well he might do.

Hugh is standing by the window: Stephen opens it from the outside and sticks his pistol through at Hugh's head.

Stephen	We meet again, Colonel.
Woman	Your tea's ready.
Stephen	Oh thanks very much.
Hugh	You went outside the game zone. You broke the rules.
Stephen	In combat there are no rules. Except survival.
Hugh	All right then.

Hugh drops his water pistol.

Stephen	That's better. Now then. Very slowly reach out and pass me my cup of tea. By the handle, Colonel.
Hugh	Very well.

Hugh makes as if to do so, but grabs his wife round the neck, holding a large knife to her neck.

One false move and the woman gets it.

Stephen	Oh come come, Colonel.
Hugh	I mean it. Drop your weapon.
Stephen	How do I know that she isn't a gook?

40

Hugh   She's not a gook.

Woman   I'm not a gook.

Hugh   There you are. So come on. Throw down your weapon.

Stephen   No. I call your bluff, Colonel.

Hugh   I'm serious.

Stephen   Off you go then.

Hugh suddenly cuts her throat: lots of blood: she falls to the floor.

Er . . . looks like you've killed your wife.

Hugh   It's only a game. *(Pause)* Isn't it?

VOX
POP

Stephen   I'm not really interested in clothes. Not really. As long as they get me from A to B.

Small Talk

Stephen addresses the loyal audience.

Stephen   When I was nine, oh fewer years ago now than
I care to remember, hum, hum! my mother told
me that in this life one could either be an elf or
a pixie. What she meant by that, I fully suppose
you may be able all too readily to guess. But her
remarks set me thinking and from that moment
on I purposed to be worthy of her admonitions
and advisalments. I suppose I can look back
on my whole life as a kind of quest, a search, a
hunt, an interrogation if you like. Yesterday was
my birthday, I won't tell you which, because I
hate you, and I celebrated it in fine style, in the
company of a cold bottle of Chablis and a couple
of prostitutes. I suppose in a sense my quest has
come full circle, OR RATHER, my hunt is over
and I can rest now. Goodnight.

VOX
POP

Stephen   Well I personally think that
the nineties will be the decade
in which masturbation really
takes off.

Dammit 2

Hugh and Stephen are in an office. Hugh is finishing a phone conversation.

Hugh   Right. Much obliged for your time, Keith.

Puts phone down.

Dammit.

Stephen   What?

Hugh   It's pretty much as we feared, John.

Stephen   Yeah?

Hugh   Only a whole heap worse.

Stephen   Suppose you start from the beginning.

Hugh   Not much to say. Seems that twenty minutes ago, our time, Derwent Enterprises went into liquidation.

Stephen   What?

Hugh   Keith called a couple of hours ago from Helsinki.

Stephen   But that was Keith just now, wasn't it?

Hugh   Yeah, just now our time. But he called a couple of hours ago his time.

Stephen   I see. And he called to say that Derwent has gone under?

Hugh   That's right.

Stephen   Damn!

Hugh   Damn it to damnation!

Stephen	Damn, blast, and two extra slices of buttered damn. Who else knows about it?
Hugh	It'll be all round town before you can say 'Hell and double-blast, dammit to Hades twice.'
Stephen	Hell and double-blast, dammit to Hades . . .

The phone rings. Hugh picks it up.

Hugh	Yes.

He hangs up.

Derek knows.

Stephen	Dammit.
Hugh	If they pull on their options . . . Christ it doesn't bear thinking about. This whole health club could go belly up.
Stephen	Right. I want to know who's behind them, I want to know who's pulling the strings, I want to know WHAT IN HELL'S NAME IS GOING ON.
Hugh	John, I do believe you're scared.
Stephen	You're damned right I'm scared, Peter. I sense Marjorie's hand in this.
Hugh	Marjorie?
Stephen	I never told you this, Peter, but when Marjorie left me I settled a block of shares on her and the boy.
Hugh	Shares in the health club? Were you out of your goddammed mind?
Stephen	In the club, no. I knew I couldn't trust her there. But I gave her shares in D-Tec.
Hugh	And you think . . .
Stephen	Think? I don't think anything. There isn't time to think. There's only time to act.

44

Hugh	But is Marjorie really capable of pulling a scrimshaw trick like this?
Stephen	*(Bitter laugh)* Marjorie? She would float her own grandmother as a holding corporation, and strip her clean of preference stock if she thought it would hurt me.

Stephen picks up a framed photo of Marjorie and her son.

Three pints of damn and a chaser of hellblast!!

Hugh	What about the boy, John?
Stephen	The boy's Dennis, Peter.
Hugh	No. What about the boy. . . . John.
Stephen	Leave the boy out of this, Peter. He's only a boy.
Hugh	Something I've always wondered, John.
Stephen	Yeah?
Hugh	How come the boy has been living with Marjorie since the divorce?
Stephen	Hih. The court ruled that I was violent and unstable, an unfit father.
Hugh	You, John? That's a damned laugh. If they had seen the way you've parented this company . . .
Stephen	Well, Marjorie told this story . . . one night I came home, I was tired, there was something about the way she looked at me, I sensed a mocking, a sneering . . . I dunno, anyway I flipped . . . emptied a bowl of trifle over her pretty little head.
Hugh	And she got custody.
Stephen	Very.
Hugh	John, it must hurt, not being able to watch Dennis grow up.

Stephen	Hurt? No. He's nothing to me now.
Hugh	Oh yeah, John? So how come every year on his birthday you take him down to London to see *Phantom of the Opera*?
Stephen	I do that because I hate him.
Hugh	Fair enough.
Stephen	But I give Marjorie due warning . . . if she wants a fight, then by God she's going to get one!
Hugh	And the prize, John?
Stephen	As big as they get, Peter. The entire leisure market in the Uttoxeter catchment area goes to the winner. No strings attached.

Picks up photo of Marjorie.

Why can't you leave me alone?

Hugh	John, what was it you once said to me about perspective?
Stephen	Er . . . I seem to remember asking you how it was spelt. . . .
Hugh	No no, after that.
Stephen	What are you saying to me, Peter?
Hugh	I'm saying, John, I'm saying, I'm saying . . . dammit I'm saying *I'm* here, Marjorie's a hundred and fifty miles away her time, if we can't fight this bastard son of a mongrel bitch then we aren't the team who weathered the Babylex crisis and came up smelling of roses. That's what I'm saying.
Stephen	Peter, you're right. Call Ipswich now, your time and tell them Derwent Enterprises or no Derwent Enterprises this Health Club is in business and stays in business.
Hugh	And if Marjorie should call?

Stephen   Marjorie? Never heard of her.

Hugh   Dammit John, I love you when you're flying.

Stephen speaks into an intercom.

Stephen   Sarah, bring in a pot of hot strong coffee and a dozen memo pads. *(Intercom off)* Now, let's get the hell out of here before they arrive.

VOX
POP

Hugh   I don't really believe in all this fuss about clouds of radioactive dust. It'll all blow over before long, I'm sure of it.

Flushed Grollings

The set is one of those warehousey sort of places, where the merchandise is behind the assistant who wears a brown warehouse coat. Lots of blue plastic trays with pro-ey looking bits and pieces.

Stephen enters with a list.

Hugh   Help you, sir?

Stephen   Um, a dozen grollings please.

Hugh   Flushed or galvanised?

Stephen   Flushed.

Hugh   Right. That be it?

Stephen   A copper flange-pipe, braced, two jubilees, seven nipples . . .

Hugh   Greased?

Stephen   Greased nipples, yeah. Five olive-spantles, jigged and onioned.

Hugh   Twelve or seventeen mill?

Stephen   Twelve. Metre of fleeling wire, coaxial, twenty UJ's and a parping couplet.

Hugh   Male or female?

Stephen   Male. No, second thoughts, one of each.

Hugh   Do you want the parping couplet standing proud?

Stephen   No, embarrassed I think.

Hugh   An embarrassed parping couplet. That it?

Stephen	Two rolls of spowling tape.
Hugh	Double-sided?
Stephen	Do they do single-sided?
Hugh	Only in Viennese lengths.
Stephen	Better go with double then. Six sheets of gruddock paper.
Hugh	Parkinised?
Stephen	No.
Hugh	Right.
Stephen	Nearly there. Four felching pens and a bevelled spill-trunion.
Hugh	Only got one felching pen left. Got some frotting pencils though.
Stephen	Will they do?
Hugh	Well, you know the thrush-plate?
Stephen	Yeah.
Hugh	You can use a frotting pencil on that, rude to the look-out valve on the fumpspoke and you can cut out the felching altogether. As long as you rim the satchel-arm properly first.
Stephen	Right. Four frotting pencils then.
Hugh	So, that's it, is it?
Stephen	Yup.
Hugh	You've already got a clip-jawed double lock brace have you?
Stephen	Do you reckon I'll need one?
Hugh	Well, are you going straight or curved?
Stephen	Straight, then curved.

49

| Hugh | Ah. Well you should be all right then, as long as you remember to suck the clenching pin tight to the arc thrust. |

Stephen slaps Hugh in the face.

| Stephen | How dare you. |
| Hugh | Sorry. |

VOX
POP

| Stephen | *(As woman)* I had shares in Gas, Electricity, Water, the lot. But then the government sold them all. |

Rosina

Stephen is in the drawing room of a stately home. He plays an old aristocratic dowager called Rosina, Lady Madding.

Stephen   I live here alone in what, when I was a girl, used to be called the Dower House. I suppose I am technically a dowager, though my son Rufus, the fourth earl, is not yet married. I love the country, it's very peaceful here. I am surrounded by photographs of my past. On the piano I have a photograph of myself dancing with David, the Prince of Wales – later of course Edward the Eighth and subsequent Duke of Windsor. David was a very bad dancer, always trod on one's toes and I remember he once crushed the metatarsal bones in the foot of a girlfriend of mine – discreet lesbianism was fashionable at the time. Here's a photograph of Noël Coward – darling Noël as we always called him. He was a very witty man, you know – it's a side of him not many people are perhaps aware of. I recall an occasion when I came onto the dance-floor of Mario's in Greek Street wearing a very daring frock, very low-cut, a frock that revealed more of my décolletage than was then considered proper – now of course I dare say it would raise nothing more than an eyebrow – but at the time it was very wicked. I came onto the floor and darling Noël came up to me and said 'Rosina,' – he always used to call me Rosina – it is my name, you must understand. 'Rosina,' he said in that voice of his, 'Rosina, where did you find such an alluringly high-cut body?' This was Noël's little way, you see. The portrait above the fireplace was made

51

when I was in Paris – Claude my husband was
Ambassador in the late 20s and I used to hold
very literary parties at the embassy – Plum and
Duff Cooper, Scott and Garrett Fitzgerald,
darling Geoffrey Chaucer of course, Adolf Hitler
and Unity Mitford, Gertrude Stein and Alice
B. Topless, Radclyffe Hall and Angela Brazil –
they could always be relied upon to attend. And
of course O. Henry James Joyce Carey Grant. I
remember F.E. Smith, later Lord Birkenhead
of course, *(Pointing, but we stay on Stephen)* that's
his picture there, just below the dartboard,
F.E. used to say 'All the world and his live-in
lover go to Rosina's parties' which pleased me
very much. Later when Claude and I went to
India to take up the Vice-regency I met Gandhi
with whom I used to play French cricket – he
was awfully good at cricket, as a matter of fact,
Claude always used to say 'what the loin-cloth
trade gained, the wicket-keeping trade lost.'
Pandit Nehru was very impressive too, though if
Edwina Mountbatten is to be believed his length
was too variable for him ever to enter the ranks
of Indian leg-spin immortals. The large bronze
statue of the nude male which stands on top of
the synthesizer is of Herbert Morrison the Cabinet
Minister. I use it to hang my bracelets on when
I'm playing at the keyboard now. I spend a lot of
time here in this room, remembering the past.
Silly Poles Hartley, L.P. Hartley, you know, once
said that the past is a foreign country, but I don't
agree. The food was better for a start, and the
people didn't *smell*. People often tell me I was
one of a spoilt generation, rich, beautiful, idle,
parasitical. It is true that I had every conceivable
luxury lavished upon me during my life, met
many famous and influential people, saw many
exciting places and never did anything more
taxing than organise large house-parties. But

you know, despite that, if I had my time over again I wouldn't change a thing. Regrets? A few. I shouldn't have let dear T.E. Lawrence borrow my motorbicycle. I'm tired now. Let me rest.

VOX
POP

Hugh   Now Kenneth Baker, it seems to me, is a perfect argument for why one should always try and kill Kenneth Baker.

Rhodes Boysons

Caption   'The Rhodes Boysons Hour'

*Stephen and Hugh are both dressed and made-up
to look like Rhodes Boyson the popular and absurd
Conservative member of parliament.*

Stephen   Hello there, I am Rhodes Boyson.

Hugh   Good evening. My name is Rhodes Boyson.

Stephen   We are the Rhodes Boysons. And this is our hour.

Hugh   This is very much our hour. An hour in which
phrases ...

Stephen   Certainly phrases ... phrases yes, certainly.

Hugh   Phrases like 'centres of excellence' will be much in
evidence.

Stephen   You will find, in this our hour, that phrases
comparable to, congruent with and exigent under,
'centres of excellence' will be, to some extent,
utilised.

Hugh   And by a centre of excellence we mean ...

Stephen   We mean, primarily ...

Hugh   Primarily that is ...

Stephen   A centre that is ...

Hugh   By and large.

Stephen   By-ly and large-ly.

Hugh   Excellent. In some regard.

Stephen   In some regard or other.

Hugh   In some, or other, regard.

54

Stephen	That is what we mean when we say 'centre of excellence'. I hope that's cleared that one up.
Hugh	Absolutely. Another phrase meaning 'centre of excellence' might be 'school that is quite good'.
Stephen	That is substantially correct in essence. A centre of excellence is a school that is quite good. But the phrase 'school that is quite good' doesn't sound nearly as . . .
Hugh	Ludicrous?
Stephen	Nearly as . . .
Hugh	Pompous?
Stephen	The phrase 'school that is quite good' doesn't sound as ludicrous or pompous as the phrase 'centre of excellence'.
Hugh	And for that reason . . .
Stephen	And that reason alone.
Hugh	We will be using the phrase 'centre of excellence' throughout our hour.
Stephen	Our hour.
Hugh	Another word that can't be stressed enough is 'standards'.
Stephen	Standards as in 'standards of excellence', moral standards, standards of accountability.
Hugh	I like that one. Standards of accountability.
Stephen	Rolls off the tongue, doesn't it? Standards of accountability.
Hugh	So for the time being, we'll leave you with those two. 'Centres of excellence'.
Stephen	That's centres of excellence.
Hugh	And 'Standards of accountability'.

Stephen Standards of accountability. Ooh, I do like that one. I shall be using that in bed tonight. Standards of accountability. Lovely.

Hugh Really quite lovely.

Stephen Perfectly lovely.

Hugh So until the next time, it's goodbye from Rhodes Boyson.

Stephen And it's goodbye from Rhodes Boyson.

Both Goodbye.

VOX
POP

Stephen *(As woman)* If you lick the top bit, very slowly, you get arrested.

Major Donaldson

A German castle. Stephen, as Major Donaldson, is slumped over a desk. Hugh is looking at a painting on the wall, his back turned towards Stephen.

Stephen stirs to some kind of consciousness.

Hugh   *(Still not looking at Stephen)* Ah, we return to some form of consciousness, Major.

Stephen   Who ... whirr ...

Hugh   You must forgive the rough methods of my colleagues. They are barbarians, barbarians. No finesse, it grieves me to say.

Stephen   Where the hell am I?

Hugh is inspecting another painting.

Hugh   You admire Matisse, Major? Such bold strokes of the brush, such masterly control. What were you doing so far in front of your lines, Major? What was the nature of your operation?

Stephen   Donaldson, Eric, Major. Serial number 46589320.

Hugh   Come, come, Major Donaldson, you can do better than that, you know. Really so much better.

Stephen   That's all you'll get out of me.

Hugh   *(Still hasn't faced Stephen)* Such a pity our two nations were ever at war. We have a great deal in common you know. *(Swings round)* Tell me please when exactly is planned your invasion of France?

Stephen   *(Looking down)* Do you think I know and do you think if I *did* know *(He looks up)* I'd ... tell ... you ... oh my God!

57

Hugh	Yes what is the matter please?
Stephen	You . . . I can't believe it!
Hugh	You are not believing what, please?
Stephen	You! You're so . . . so beautiful!
Hugh	What are you saying?
Stephen	I can't . . . this is . . . oh my God, this is it! Who'd've believed it? Here? Now? You're just the most fantastic, the loveliest creature I've ever set eyes on.
Hugh	Don't play games with me, Major Donaldson. I'm not very good at them.
Stephen	Games? Games? This is no game! This is the reallest thing that's ever happened to me. I just don't . . . where the hell have you been all my life, you fabulous darling?
Hugh	Now look . . .
Stephen	Oh God there's so much I want to know . . . your name, I don't even know what he's called . . . God, we've so much lost time to make up for.

Stephen turns round a name card on Hugh's desk. It reads in Gothic upper case 'Oberleutnant Friedrich von Stoltz'.

Friedrich! Yes, Friedrich! it suits you.

Hugh	Have you taken leave of your senses?
Stephen	Yes! Yes, Friedie, I have! For the first time in my life I have taken leave of my senses, and I love it! Did anyone ever tell you you have the sweetest, silliest little nose . . . and the biggest bluest eyes?

Hugh turns angrily away.

Hugh	I give you one last warning, Major Donaldson!

Stephen	Get that arse! That has got to be the cutest little bum *ever!*
Hugh	*(Furious by now)* No, now this is enough! Enough you hear?! Perhaps you are trying on me some of your English senses of humour, but I tell you ...
Stephen	And the accent, it's just so *dreamy!*
Hugh	WHEN IS PLANNED THE INVASION?
Stephen	Oh, who cares about the stupid little invasion, Friedrich honey-puss? July the third, three beach-heads on Normandy codenamed Omaha, Utah and Nebraska, I think. But what does that matter? What matters is that we've found each other.
Hugh	Normandy?
Stephen	Normandy. Now, don't you think that deserves a kiss?
Hugh	Well, maybe just a little one.

VOX
POP

Stephen	There was a very famous writer once, I can't actually remember who it was, but he was once asked by a hotel porter for his name, and he said 'G.K. Chesterton'. I think it might have been Oscar Wilde.

Spies/Pulse

Hugh enters Control's office. Stephen appears to be taking his own pulse.

Hugh Hello, Control. *(No reply)* Control? Are you all right? You appear to be taking your pulse.

Stephen I am a Russian spy, Tony. That's what I am.

Hugh I beg your pardon?

Stephen I plan to overthrow the Queen.

Hugh Control, this is a bit of a surprise. All the more so because you're actually the head of British Intelligence.

Stephen I aim to undermine the entire Western way of life.

Hugh Mmm. Before you do that, I'll go and telephone the relevant authorities. And as a precaution, please don't open any more letters.

Stephen No, it's all right Murchison. I'm not really a Russian spy.

Hugh Now Control. You mustn't say that just to spare me the paperwork.

Stephen No honestly, Tony, I'm really not a Russian spy. And you were right, by the way. I was taking my pulse.

Hugh I thought as much. Because you were gripping your wrist lightly but firmly and counting to yourself.

Stephen You see, our American counterparts have invented a new machine called a lie-detector, that lets you know you when people are telling you fibs.

60

Hugh	Surely that would be rather useful for people in our line of work, Control?
Stephen	Exactly, Tony. The machine works on the well-known scientific principle that when someone's telling you a fib, their pulse speeds up.
Hugh	Gosh, Control, how incredibly ingenious but at the same time how quite simple.
Stephen	Sadly however, these machines are rather expensive to buy.
Hugh	Oh dear. Our American counterparts do often seem to have lots more money to spend than we do, don't they, Control?
Stephen	Yes, but what they have in money, I like to think we make up for in British know-how.
Hugh	I'm not quite following, Control.
Stephen	Well, Tony, at a fraction of the cost I have come up with this lie-detector.
	Indicates (stop-watch).
Hugh	A stop-watch, of course! It cuts out the need for expensive and cumbersome equipment.
Stephen	When I told you I was a Russian spy, I was telling a deliberate fib.
Hugh	Ah. You wanted to see if your pulse got faster?
Stephen	That's right.
Hugh	Did it?
Stephen	No.
Hugh	Oh dear. If your pulse didn't speed up, that must mean . . .
Stephen	Yes. When I said I was a Russian spy, I must have been telling the truth.

Hugh	Mm. So on the very first try of this technique you've discovered that you, the Head of British Intelligence, are a Soviet agent.
Stephen	That's right. And Tony?
Hugh	Control?
Stephen	The £9.50 that it cost me to buy that stop-watch turns out to have been money well-spent.
Hugh	Gosh, Control. The implications of your discovery are considerable.
Stephen	Aren't they, Murchison? The Minister will be ever so pleased.
Hugh	Mmm. Don't you think we ought to test the technique again, just to make sure?
Stephen	Good idea. We don't want to go round boasting that we've discovered that I'm a top level Russian spy unless we're absolutely certain.
Hugh	My thoughts exactly, Control.
Stephen	All right, Tony, you tell me a fib, and I'll see if your pulse goes up.

Stephen takes Hugh's pulse.

| Hugh | Hmm. Let's see if I can think of something that isn't true. Oh yes, I know. My name is Susan Donovan. |

Pause. Stephen counts and then withdraws his hand.

Stephen	Well, that seems to prove it.
Hugh	Really?
Stephen	Yes, Susan, really.
Hugh	Mm. *(Pause)* Control?
Stephen	Yes, Susan?
Hugh	Why don't we go back to our old way?

Stephen   You mean . . .?

Hugh   Yes. The good old British Secret Service method of finding out if someone is telling you a fib or not.

Stephen   All right. You first. Is your name Tony Murchison?

Hugh   *(Holding up hand)* Yes. Cub's Honour.

Stephen   My turn.

Hugh   Are you a Russian spy?

Stephen   I am not a Russian spy, cross my heart and hope to die.

Hugh   Phew!

Stephen   Glad we're all sorted out again.

Hugh   Me too! You know what, Control?

Stephen   What, Tony?

Hugh   I'm going to bring you a cup of nice coffee now . . .

Makes to leave. Stops and smiles at Control.

. . . and that's the truth!

Stephen   Boh!

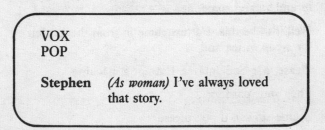

VOX
POP

Stephen   *(As woman)* I've always loved that story.

Anal Retention

Hugh is on a couch. Stephen sits beside him.

Stephen   So, Mr Sedelmayer, you believe yourself to be
          anally retentive?

Hugh   Not half.

Stephen   Not half. No, I imagine not half. Now
          anal retentiveness is a complex condition,
          Mr Sedelmayer. What gave you the idea that you
          were suffering from this problem?

Hugh   A book.

Stephen   A book? Well, well, well, well, well. A book on
          psychiatry?

Hugh   First World War Biplanes.

Stephen   First World War Biplanes. It was a book on First
          World War Biplanes that led you to believe that
          you were anally retentive?

Hugh   That's right.

Stephen   Mm. I must say I can't pretend to understand you
          – not without going to Drama School and taking
          an expensive course of lessons in how to pretend
          to understand someone.

Hugh   Well it's like this. I'd just come in from the garden
          for a cup of tea and ...

Stephen   Please, Mr Sedelmayer, I'm not a machine.

Hugh   I beg your pardon?

Stephen   A little slower, if you please.

Hugh   Oh right. I sat down on this chair ...

Stephen	Well, get on with it.
Hugh	Right. I sat down on this chair.
Stephen	This chair?
Hugh	No, no. The chair in my kitchen. And as I sat down, I noticed that on the chair was this book all about First World War Biplanes and I sat down and had a cup of tea, nice cup of tea, very nice, the tea wasn't the problem, no sir, the problem was that when I got up I noticed that the book wasn't there.
Stephen	Yes?
Hugh	It wasn't anywhere, you see. It had vanished. That's when I realised that I'd retained it.
Stephen	You'd retained it.
Hugh	Correct.
Stephen	Anally?
Hugh	Of course anally. Of course. What other explanation could there be?
Stephen	You tell me, Mr Sedelmayer.
Hugh	No.
Stephen	All right. Now this chair. Describe it to me.
Hugh	Oh you know, a chair. A kiitchen chair. Made in Hungary.
Stephen	A Hungarian kitchen chair. My oh my. And where is this chair now?
	Pause.
	Where is this chair now?
Hugh	Isn't it obvious? I sat down again, you see, because I was shocked by the disappearance of the book on First World War Biplanes, and when I got up . . .

Stephen	No chair?
Hugh	Vanished. Gone.
Stephen	Retained . . . by you . . .
Hugh	Anally.
Stephen	Anally. Yes. I see. So the disappearance of a book on First World War Biplanes and a Hungarian kitchen chair have forced you to the conclusion . . .
Hugh	Oh they're not all.
Stephen	Oh lordy Belgrano. You mean there's more?
Hugh	Much more. Look out of the window.
Stephen	Mr Sedelmayer, I am a man of science, I haven't time to look out of windows.
Hugh	Please.
Stephen	Very well.
Hugh	I came here today by car.
Stephen	Yes?
Hugh	I've never been one for public transport. Too many germs. I came here today in a blue Vauxhall Carlton, purchased from Howden, the Used Car Dealers, for a pretty sum . . .
Stephen	On the Bardon Road?
Hugh	That's it. Big place, with a lot of cars. They're dear, mind, but they give you peace of mind.
Stephen	And you can't put a price on that.
Hugh	Well, £6,299 was the price they managed to put on it.
Stephen	Right, yes. Good, excellent. So you came in your Carlton, parked . . .

66

Hugh	Exactly. I parked, got out of the vehicle, turned round to effect the security procedure . . .
Stephen	To wit . . . ?
Hugh	To wit, locking the door . . . and what do you think met my gaze?
Stephen	Nothing?
Hugh	You've got it in one. The blue Vauxhall Carlton had, in effect, been retained by me.
Stephen	I see.
Hugh	So I suppose what I'm asking in my stumbling, hopeless fashion is, what can I do?
Stephen	Well it wouldn't hurt to take the bus just once . . .
Hugh	No, no, no. You misunderstand me for comic effect. I mean what am I to do about my anal retentiveness?
Stephen	Well now, Mr Sedelmayer, I could lie to you. It would be ridiculously easy just to tell you a lot of lies . . . in fact that's what I think I'll do. You're fine, Mr Sedelmayer, you've got absolutely nothing to worry about.
Hugh	Goodness me, that's a relief.
Stephen	And if you're worried about your car –
Hugh	Not particularly, it was insured.
Stephen	Oh that's all right then. I was going to suggest a couple of pints of kaolin and morphine and a bowl of prunes, but if it's insured . . .

Over To You

Stephen plays Colin Essdale, a drama producer, Hugh plays a complaining woman called Mary Barratt. The presenter is called Elspeth.

Hugh   Well I thought it was disgusting. The whole thing was disgusting.

Elspeth   Yes, did . . .

Hugh   There was no warning of what was in store, none whatever . . .

Elspeth   To be fair, the . . .

Hugh   And for goodness sake what about my children? No thought was given to this at all.

Elspeth   Did your children see the . . .?

Hugh   No they didn't. They didn't see it. But only thanks to the purest good fortune that they don't happen to have been born yet, otherwise I dread to think what damage may have been caused. It was simply disgusting.

Elspeth   Yes, the . . .

Hugh   Simply disgusting.

Pause. Elspeth thinks that Hugh has stopped.

Elspeth   Turning to you Mr . . .

Hugh   Simply disgusting.

Elspeth   Mm. Colin Essdale, as the producer, what do . . .?

Stephen   *(Nodding caringly)* Mm. Mm. Mm. Mm. This is obviously difficult . . . mm . . . perhaps it would help if I explained that I couldn't give a flying toss about Mrs Barratt or her feeble views.

Elspeth	Er, well the . . .
Hugh	I beg your pardon?
Stephen	Now, if you don't mind, or even if you do . . . I have only an estimated 45 years left on this planet and I don't propose to waste a further second of them talking to a confused old gasbag like you.
Elspeth	Well, on the other hand . . .
Stephen	*(Unhooks tie-mike à la John Nott)* So, I'm off to see a colleague about making a programme which I fully hope will irritate you and your half-wit friends even more than the last one. Bye!
	Exit Stephen.
Elspeth	So, Mrs Barratt are you satisfied with what you've heard?
Hugh	Well not really, no.
Elspeth	Tough. *(Shouting off)* A last word from you, Mr Essdale?
	Stephen re-enters with drink.
Stephen	Pim-hole.

VOX
POP

Hugh The people of Berlin are doing very exciting things with the city at the moment. Basically they had this idea of just knocking it through into one.

Grandfather's Things

Stephen   I was just sorting through my grandfather's old
hairdriers the other day, when I came across this,
wedged in the filter of an old Pifco Easy Tress
Ultramatic.

Holds up a small piece of paper.

It's a letter addressed to my grandfather from
the then Minister of Housing, Ernest Dalloway,
later of course Lord Dalloway of Spalding. I'll
read it to you, if I may. 'Your letter to the Home
Secretary has been passed on to me, as Minister in
charge of urban development. I dream of covering
your upturned face with a thousand burning
kisses . . .' and there's a bit more like that . . .
but, oh yes here we are . . . this is the good bit,
'I would direct your attention to Section 17 of the
Housing Act (Urban) 1916, paragraph 5: "Where
a local authority has given no other sanction," you
furious ball of shining beauty, blah, blah blah, "the
entitlement to grants under the scheme will come
mandatorily into operation," please, please let me
stroke your thigh. I hope this answers your enquiry
in the matter of 14 Stanshall Avenue, I yearn to
drink clarified butter from your armpits, etc etc
etc Ernest Dalloway.' Fascinating little glimpse of
history, there, I think.

Stunts

Stephen   Ladies and gentlemen, many of you have expressed the worry that some of what Hugh and I do in this show is physically very dangerous, and have asked whether or not we ever use stuntmen in the performance of our sketches.

Hugh   Well the answer is basically that Stephen and I do all our own stunts.

Stephen   All our own stunts.

Hugh   Every single one.

Stephen   And almost none of our own acting.

Hugh   That's right. It's not widely known, but acting is in fact an incredibly dangerous thing to do . . .

Stephen   Incredibly dangerous, and for insurance reasons we have been forbidden from delivering all but the simplest lines.

Cut to Stephen and Hugh 'in performance' while their voices continue off . . .

Hugh   *(Voice-over)* Take for example this sketch, that we're about to record now. It's called 'The Adventures Of Colin The Serving Hatch', and it begins with me diving through a plate-glass window, with my bottom on fire.

Hugh dives through a window, trousers ablaze.

Stephen   *(Voice-over)* Those of you who are doing this sketch for A-Level will know that the next thing is for me to smash Hugh in the face with a cricket bat . . .

Hugh   *(Voice-over)* Whereupon I crash through a wall and fall on to some iron railings.

In vision, the relevant actions can be seen. Somebody shouts 'cut' and Stephen steps in and addresses the camera.

Stephen Now comes the really dangerous bit – the first line. And to do this line, we've drafted in Alan Witheridge, who has almost twenty years experience of delivering lines like this one. Alan is going to 'double' for Hugh at this point in the sketch, and say the line 'I'm so sorry, I thought you were my brother.'

We can see Alan preparing for the line. Kneepads etc. Stephen goes over to interview him.

Alan, how's it going?

Alan Fine thanks, Stephen. Just putting the final touches to the preparation.

Stephen Are you nervous at a time like this?

Alan Not nervous, no. If you've done your homework, which I think I have, there should be no problem. Anyway, we'll see.

Stephen Well Alan, the very best of luck.

Alan takes up his position in the set. A voice shouts 'stand by'.

(Voice-over) Just to remind you that Alan is now going to try and say the line, 'I'm so sorry I thought you were my brother.' Fingers crossed.

A voice shouts 'action' and Alan begins.

Alan I'm so sorry, I thought . . .

Alan explodes and people run in with fire extinguishers.

Stephen Well, a lucky escape for Hugh there.

Wrong directions

Hugh Good evening and welcome to 'Realising I've Given The Wrong Directions To'. Tonight I shall be Realising I've Given The Wrong Directions to Rabbi Michael Leibovitz. Sadly, Rabbi Leibovitz is unable to be with us tonight. Till next time, bye bye.

VOX
POP

Stephen Margaret Thatcher is the best thing that's ever happened to this country.

Mountaineer

A hotel bar at the foot of Ben Enormous. Stephen is the bartender, with a ludicrously long beard, Hugh is a git.

Hugh	Oh she's beautiful, isn't she?
Stephen	She?
Hugh	The mountain.
Stephen	Ah.
Hugh	I always think of the mountain as 'she'. To me, the mountain will always be 'she'.
Stephen	I know what you mean.
Hugh	Do you? Yes, I think perhaps you do.
Stephen	But to me, you see, the mountain is an 'it'.
Hugh	An 'it'.
Stephen	'It', yes. To me, the mountain has always had an 'itty' sort of quality.
Hugh	Interesting.
Stephen	I think of my wife as a 'she'.
Hugh	Is that right?
Stephen	Oh yes. I always think of my wife as being a woman. Does that sound mad?
Hugh	Mad? No, it's not mad. Your wife as a woman. Interesting.
Stephen	Well, romantic, perhaps. You married?
Hugh	Yes indeed. Oh yes. Marriage is a wonderful thing. It's upstairs at the moment. It's a bit tired after the journey.
Stephen	'It'?

74

Hugh	My wife.
Stephen	Oh I see. I thought you meant the mountain. I thought you meant the mountain was upstairs.
Hugh	No no no.
Stephen	So are you going to be climbing tomorrow?
Hugh	Oh yes. I shall be up her face tomorrow morning, first thing.
Stephen	With your wife?
Hugh	Oh no. It's never really enjoyed climbing. It doesn't like heights, you see. Mind you, neither do I.
Stephen	Then why do you climb? That sounds very odd. It sounds very strange indeed.
Hugh	It is strange, it's mad really. I can't think why I married it. That's why I climb mountains, I suppose. To get away from it.
Stephen	And of course you're so beautiful.
Hugh	I beg your pardon?
Stephen	You are so ravishingly lovely.
Hugh	Well that's very kind of you I'm sure.
Stephen	Wales, that is. I always think of Wales as a 'you'. Don't know why.
Hugh	Oh, I understand. Yes, you certainly are lovely, aren't you?
Stephen	Oh yes. What a great country you are.

Drifting through the window we hear a lilting Welsh hymn.

Hugh	Ah. You hear that? What a beautiful hymn.
Stephen	Ah. You think of that as a him, do you? That's funny, because I'd call that a 'they'. To me, that's a beautifully sung 'they'.

75

Hugh	Ah, it's pure poetry, isn't it?
Stephen	Your wife? Your wife is poetry?
Hugh	No, the hymn is poetry.
Stephen	Well I don't know. I don't think they is poetry. I always think that poetry is poetry.
Hugh	You're talking now of Dylan Thomas.
Stephen	Dylan Thomas, yes . . . or any of the other great poets, like . . .
Hugh	Dylan Thomas.
Stephen	Yes and . . . er . . .
Hugh	Dylan Thomas.
Stephen	Coal black . . .
Hugh	Black as black . . .
Stephen	Slow black . . .
Hugh	Black . . .
Stephen	Black . . . Aye.
Hugh	I?
Stephen	Yes. I always think of aye as yes. Yes, there's no doubt about it, we're very, very lucky.
Hugh	We?
Stephen	The Welsh. I always think of the Welsh as 'we'. A great stream of we.
Hugh	Yes, a huge reservoir of we, I know what you mean.
Stephen	Oh Wales, you're so lovely.
Hugh	You certainly are. I'd live there if the bastards didn't keep burning down my holiday cottage.

Dammit 3

Hugh is on the phone in the boardroom. Stephen enters and throws off his coat. Hugh nods a greeting.

Hugh   *(Looking at his watch)* Dammit to blue-rinsed Hades!

Stephen   Problem, Peter?

Hugh   *(Hangs up)* Yeah. This watch keeps losing time, John. It was a birthday gift from Nancy and I haven't the heart to tell her that it keeps time about as well as a Rangoon stevedore. So tell me John, how did the meeting go?

Stephen   I don't know how the meeting went, Peter.

Hugh   I don't understand, John.

Stephen   It's very simple, Peter. I didn't go.

Hugh   You didn't go, John? I understand even less . . .

Stephen   Would it help if I told you that Marjorie was at the meeting, Peter?

Hugh   Marjorie?

Stephen   Check. With her two lap-poodles, Dexter and O'Neill.

Hugh   What the deuce was that hell-bitch Marjorie doing there?

Stephen   Marjorie is a majority stockholder in Barraclough Leisure, Peter. She's entitled to attend any damned meeting she chooses.

Hugh   Oh come on, John. Marjorie holds stock in just about every major leisure corporation in the Uttoxeter *Yellow Pages*. Are you telling me . . .?

Stephen	I don't know what I'm telling you, Peter. But I decided there and then that if Marjorie and I were going to war, it would be on the ground of my choosing . . .
Hugh	But dammit, John . . .
Stephen	Wait a minute, I haven't finished.
Hugh	Sorry, John.
Stephen	It would be on the ground of my choosing . . . Peter.
Hugh	Right. But there's something else on your mind. In can tell. I've seen that look before.
Stephen	I was just thinking, how old's the boy now?
Hugh	The boy? Where does he come into this?
Stephen	Half that Barraclough stock is his, remember?
Hugh	You mean . . .?
Stephen	I mean, Peter, the boy's old enough to think for himself. If he's anything like his father he'll have a mind of his own.
Hugh	You're his father John.
Stephen	No Peter. As a matter of record, I'm not.
Hugh	This is a story I've not heard.
Stephen	*(Pouring himself a drink and staring into the distance)* It was while I was working every hour that God sent and plenty more on top of that, making something of this health club, wheeling, dealing, bobbing, weaving, ducking and diving through every centimetre of red tape the local Uttoxeter bureaucrats could tie me up with, hustling, breaking my DAMNED ARSE to set this company on the right road.
Hugh	And Marjorie wanted children.

78

Stephen	That's right. The business was just starting to turn the corner, and there was Marjorie, asking me to throw away ten minutes of my life in order to have a child. I just couldn't do that.
Hugh	I understand, but I don't understand.
Stephen	Simple. I did what any good businessman would have done in my place. I delegated. Put Tim on the case.
Hugh	Tim . . .
Stephen	Luckily he was able to fit it in. The rest, as they say, is damned history. Tim is the boy's father.
Hugh	Not strictly true, John.
Stephen	Peter? You have some input on this?
Hugh	I swear to you John, I had no idea where the brief originated, but Tim came to me one night saying that he'd bitten off more than he could chew, and could I get him out of a jam.
Stephen	Don't tell me . . .
Hugh	I'm afraid so, John. Tim delegated the delegating.
Stephen	Damn his arse! Are you telling me that you're the boy's father, Peter?
Hugh	Not as simple as that, I'm afraid. I was up to my neck with Nancy at the time. Strung out on a wire trying to set up finance for her Vegetable Boutique.
Stephen	So you delegated?
Hugh	I had no choice, John. Things were happening so fast you had to run just to keep moving.
Stephen	Come on, Peter. Who did you dump this one on?
Hugh	You're not going to like it, John.
Stephen	No . . . you can't mean? Marjorie?

79

Hugh	That's right. Marjorie. Who else could I have turned to, John?
Stephen	So Marjorie is the boy's father? That is sick.
Hugh	No no no. It gets a little bit complicated here, John. Marjorie was hustling some deal out Peterborough way, on the road day and night . . .
Stephen	Marjorie delegated? I can't believe this. Who to?
Hugh	The boy, John.
Stephen	To the boy? The boy is his own father?
Hugh	That's right. The boy is his own father.
Stephen	Seven types of executive damn with a free hellblast!
Hugh	But John, maybe this can still work for us. Maybe we can bring pressure to bear on the boy by appealing to his father.
Stephen	Get the boy to persuade himself to vote our way, you mean?
Hugh	It might work.
Stephen	What can we lose?
Both	Daamn!!

VOX
POP

Hugh   I don't think so.

Michael Jackson

Hugh is sitting in a chat show swivel chair, addressing the camera.

Hugh   Ladies and gentlemen, this is a genuinely exciting moment for me. We're extremely honoured to have on the show tonight one of those very rare performers – a man who perhaps more than any other can lay claim to the title 'superstar'. Ladies and gentlemen, will you please welcome, Michael Jackson.

Applause and music: 'Bad'. Stephen enters, shakes hands with Hugh and sits down.

Michael, thank you very much indeed for coming on the show.

Stephen   Pleasure.

Hugh   I know you must be frantically busy . . .

Stephen   Things are a bit hectic at the moment, yes.

Hugh   I believe you're about to start work on a new album?

Stephen   A new album, that's right. It's absolutely brand new. Even the little hole in the middle is new.

Hugh   I love these clothes, by the way.

Stephen   Oh thank you, yes. This is a plain Irish Thornproof, very hard wearing, I've had it for some time actually.

Hugh   I bet thousands of kids all over the world are trying to copy this look right now.

Stephen   Well haha . . . perhaps.

Hugh   Now Michael, you've been in the music business for . . . well most of your life . . .

Stephen   Just about, yes.

Hugh   Right, and of course 'Thriller' has sold more copies than any other record, you're without doubt the biggest star of this or perhaps any generation. Have you ever wondered what your life would have been like if none of this had ever happened?

Stephen   Yes. Yes, I do. There's no way of knowing this, obviously, but I sometimes think if all this hadn't happened, my life would have been very different indeed.

Hugh   Really?

Stephen   Well I think so, yes. It's so hard to know, of course.

Hugh   Now Michael, I have to ask you this. There has been some speculation over the years that you have, with the aid of plastic surgery, set about altering your appearance.

Stephen   Well I don't really pay any attention to that. That's just newspapers, you know . . .

Hugh   So you absolutely deny it?

Stephen   Well I don't think it's even worth denying. All it boils down to is people being jealous of my success. People will say anything.

Hugh   Yes. We've got a picture of you here, when you were with the Jackson Five – you'd just signed to Motown, I believe . . .

Cut to eight-year-old Michael Jackson.

You do look a bit different . . .

82

Stephen	I was eight years old, for heaven's sake. I mean of course I've changed. We've all changed.
Hugh	Absolutely. Well, Michael, I hope that's answered your critics. Now I believe you're actually going to do a song for us now from the new album?
Stephen	That's right. This song is called 'Move It On Out Girl'.
Hugh	Ladies and gentlemen – 'Move It On Out Girl' – Michael Jackson!

Stephen walks over to 'performance area' and starts grooving to the intro. He somehow gets on to an exercise treadmill to do the walking on the spot. He apparently sings.

Stephen	Move it on out girl, Don't leave it where it is, girl, Put it somewhere else, girl, Don't move it on in.

If you move it on in, girl,
I might have to find another girl,
Who'll give me less trouble girl,
Who'll move it on out . . .

Stephen does a groovy dance break, during which Hugh comes over and interrupts the song.

Sorry, is there a problem?

Hugh	No no, Michael, that was very enjoyable. It's just that I couldn't help noticing that you were miming.
Stephen	No I wasn't.
Hugh	Yes you were.
Stephen	No I wasn't.

From now on we begin to notice that Stephen is actually miming his answers to Hugh's questions.

Hugh   I mean I'm sorry, but you see I just think that this is so disappointing. It's almost impossible for the kids to see an artist doing a live performance nowadays . . .

Stephen   Look, I know some people do it, but I promise you that miming is simply not the Michael Jackson way. Atishoo!

Visually, Stephen's sneeze is about five seconds after we hear it.

Hugh   *(To camera)* It's tragic when stars don't live up to your expectations.

VOX
POP

Stephen   No, I was joking. She's as mad as a house.

Sponsored Sketch

This is shot entirely from a low level. All we see are bare legs, from the knee down.

Stephen	*(Kissing the guests)* Tom, Irene, welcome!
Hugh	Dick, thanks for inviting us.
Selina	First all-naked party I've been to for years.
Stephen	Yes, well we thought it would make a change.
Hugh	Saves the problem of having to decide what to wear anyway!
Stephen	Right!

They find this really amusing.

Selina	Nice carpet . . . is it a Tideyman's?
Stephen	Now how on earth could you tell that?
Hugh	Well I suppose it was the modern, up-to-the-minute design wasn't it darling?
Selina	And the practicability.
Stephen	I'm surprised how large your breasts are, Irene.
Selina	Why thank you. And I must say you have a very amusingly shaped . . .
Hugh	*(Interrupting)* . . . Dick, I believe I'm also right in saying that it repels stains and resists spills.
Stephen	The carpet, I hope you mean! Yes, that's right. Nothing soaks into a Tideyman's.
Hugh	I expect we'll be putting that to the test before the evening's out.
Stephen	Rather. Let me stroke your thighs, Irene.

Selina	Thanks. I have to say it's a great colour. What would you call this colour, exactly?
Stephen	Well, flesh-coloured, I suppose.
Hugh	I think Irene was referring to the Tideyman's actually.
Stephen	Oh right.
Selina	No I wasn't.
Hugh	Oh.
Selina	It's a sort of purple, really, isn't it?
Hugh	But come to think of it, what made you choose this colour of Tideyman's?
Stephen	Well it was quite difficult at first, because they had so many to choose from, but with the aid of their highly trained sales staff we finally came to the right decision.
Hugh	Seems to me you made the right decision right at the beginning.
Stephen	Oh?
Hugh	By going to Tideyman's in the first place.
Stephen	Right! Dip?
Selina	Yes, it does rather, doesn't it.

VOX
POP

Hugh   We took the caravan down to Dorset this year, and pushed it over a cliff.

A view of the Chadrot valley before engineers
began to work on the hydro-electric dam.
(The dam now provides eighty per cent
of the power used in Staffordshire brothels.)

The famous 'Squirrel Scene' from the suppressed third reel of the movie. Cameraman Geoffrey Unsworth is second from the left. Christopher Biggins has his back to camera and his head in a small basket.

The standard 'Nun's Feet' formation. Note that if player A (ringed) switches to the Corsican straddle, the formation reverts to the more usual Double Sidebreast or Inkerman Reverse.

Neddy Carter's despairing dive fails to prevent Aston Villa's smooth progression into the third round. A crowd of 29,000 saw the game.

Farmhouse cheese-making has altered little over the years in the Cotswold village of Addis Ababa. Here, the 'grilk' is separated from the 'tappy' by means of a circular 'swottle'. (The unused 'tappy' is sold on to manufacturers of car exhaust systems.)

Officers and men of Number Six Squadron, the Royal Air Force in a scene from their theatre-in-the-nude production of Rattigan's *Flare Path*.

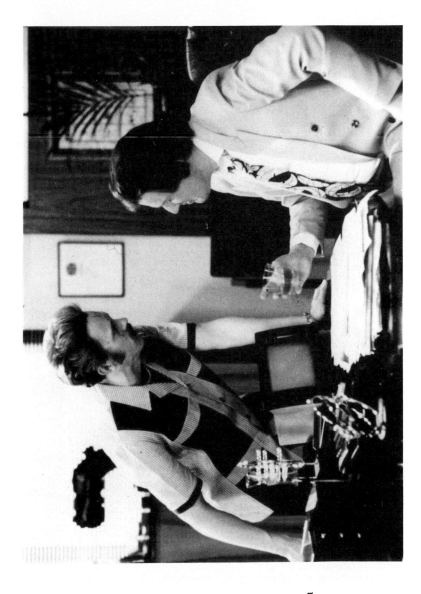

J. H. St C. L. in
happier days.
You can see the
Soane grotto in
the background
and Mamou with
her beloved
Westie terriers,
Squeakie and
Turd.

Beethoven arranca constantes sorpresas de tonalidad,
indicación y dinámica. 'Beethoven springs constant surprises
of tonality, register and dynamics.' Practise especially
an even, level intonation on the word 'indica*ción*',
being careful to masturbate gently with the left hand.

Shoplifting

Stephen is sitting at a desk in a dingy office. Hugh and a woman enter. Hugh is a supermarket security guard, she is a housewife.

Hugh   Come on, in you go.

Woman   There's no need to push. I can walk.

Stephen   Ah. Tango Four, is it?

Hugh   Sorry to bother you, Mr Turner. It looks like we've got a ten twenty-three on our hands.

Woman   Will you let go of my arm?

Stephen   A ten twenty-three, oh dear.

Woman   You have absolutely no right to keep me here.

Stephen   Won't you have a seat, Mrs . . .?

Hugh   Target responds to the name of King, sir.

Stephen   All right, Tango Four, let's have your report.

Hugh   Sir. As per your briefing instructions, I was positioned in aisle number three, between breakfast cereals and bread, operating a mobile figure of eight pattern around frozen vegetables.

Stephen   Textbook stuff, Tango Four.

Hugh   Thank you, sir. I then observed the target loitering opposite the Coco Pops.

Woman   Look, I have to pick up my children at four o'clock, so if you . . .

Stephen   What's your name. son?

Hugh   Lewis, sir. Oliver Lewis.

Stephen	This your first taste of action?
Hugh	Yes, sir.
Stephen	Quite a feeling, isn't it?
Hugh	Oh yes, sir. Quite a feeling.
Stephen	I remember my first ten twenty-three. 1968. Still had me bum fluff.
Woman	Look, I'm sorry to interrupt, but my children are waiting for me at school . . .
Stephen	My advice to you, Mrs King, is to pay a little more attention to your own problems just at the minute! *(To Hugh)* Doesn't hurt to shake 'em up a bit early on.
Hugh	It's joy to watch you, sir.
Stephen	Come come, my dear, dry those tears. Hanky?
Woman	No thank you.
Stephen	*(To Hugh)* Hard, then soft, you see?
Hugh	Beautiful, sir.
Stephen	Now then, Mrs King, I'm going to tell you a story.
Woman	Oh God.
Stephen	One day, a woman goes into a supermarket and steals some Coco Pops. Do you like my story, Mrs King?
Woman	Not really.
Stephen	I'm pretty near the mark though, aren't I?
Woman	No.
Hugh	She's lying, sir!
Stephen	All right, Lewis. I think Mrs King and I understand each other.
Woman	I don't think we do.

Stephen   After all, lifting a packet of Coco Pops isn't such a terrible thing, is it? Not when you look at what they get up to at football matches these days. No, I'd say that shoving a packet of Coco Pops down your cleavage and forgetting to pay for them is just being human, after all.

Woman   Have you finished?

Stephen   No I haven't finished, you snotsucking ball of slime.

Woman   Now look here . . .

Stephen   No, you look here. See that? Know what that means?

He points to a medal ribbon on his chest.

Woman   No.

Stephen   Tell her, laddie.

Hugh   I'm afraid I don't know either, sir.

Stephen   This is a Distinguished Service Medal, from the Arndale Centre in Chippenham!

He points to a photo on the wall.

That's me! There! Shaking hands with the manager. Read out the citation, Lewis.

Hugh   Right, sir. *(Reads)* 'Harry Turner is congratulated on his alertness in apprehending a shoulder of lamb – New Zealand.'

Stephen   Stolen lamb, Mrs King. Stolen lamb, stolen Coco Pops. Comprendo?

Woman   Are you accusing me of theft?

Stephen   Affirmatory, Mrs King!

Woman   Right. *(She rootles in her handbag)* What do you think this is? *(Takes out piece of paper)*

Hugh	Careful sir, it could be a trap.
Woman	It's a bloody receipt. *(Reads)* Coco P. 48 pence!
Stephen	Have you got a receipt for that receipt?
Woman	Of course I haven't.
Hugh	Haha!
Stephen	No, course you haven't. 'Cos you nicked it, didn't you?
Hugh	Confess, confess! You're from a broken home!
Stephen	Steady, Lewis.
Hugh	Sorry, sir.
Woman	Look, why don't we just call the police?
Stephen	Police. Hear that, Lewis?
Hugh	I did, sir. Very amusing.
Stephen	I shouldn't worry too much about the police, Mrs King.
Hugh	Police. Ha. *(Spits)*
Stephen	A fine body of men, on the whole, but amateurs when it comes to analysing the mind of a ten twenty-three. I could have joined the police if I'd wanted, Mrs King. The money's better of course, what with the housing allowance, but in the end I said to myself . . . 'Harry, my boy, you belong with the elite.'
Hugh	Good on you, sir.
Stephen	Thank you, Lewis. Or may I call you Oliver?
Hugh	I'd be honoured. Harry.
Woman	You pathetic pair of twerps.
Stephen	I'm sorry?
Woman	You sad, crappy, twerps. I'm leaving now.

Stephen   Well I'm afraid we're a long way from finishing
              yet . . .

*The woman gets to her feet. Stephen tries to stop her
but she disables him with some fancy martial artwork
and then throws Hugh across the desk. She exits looking
cool. Stephen and Hugh pick themselves up off the floor.*

Yes, you're probably wondering why I let her walk
out just like that?

Hugh   Well she was obviously innocent, sir.

Stephen   Exactly. Knew it from the start. You get a nose for
              it after a while.

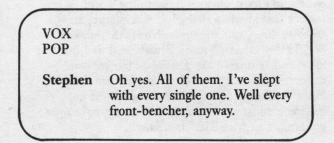

VOX
POP

Stephen   Oh yes. All of them. I've slept
              with every single one. Well every
              front-bencher, anyway.

Satire/Tribute

Stephen   Hello. Welcome to 'A Bit Of Fry And Laurie'.

Hugh   Grrrrr.

Stephen   Ladies and gentlemen, because Hugh and I are known for our anger, our satirical rage at the 'human condition', for want of a better cliché . . .

Hugh   Grrrr . . .

Stephen   We often get accused of lacking a sense of proportion. Here's a letter . . . 'It's very easy to knock, to rage and snarl and satirise, but what are you suggesting should go in the place of the institutions and people you so viciously decry?' This is a typical letter from Mr Alan Dense, absolutely typical. He writes letters like this all the time . . . 'It's oh so simple to knock Mrs Thatcher, isn't it?' Well of course he's quite right. It is ludicrously easy to knock Mrs Thatcher. It's the easiest and most obvious thing in the world to remark that she is a shameful, putrid scab, an embarrassing, ludicrous monstrosity that makes one frankly ashamed to be British, and that her ideas and standards are a stain on our national history. That's easy and clear, anyone can do that. But after tonight, no one can accuse us of not making a constructive suggestion as to what might go in place of Mrs Thatcher. Hugh.

Hugh holds up a wire coathanger.

That is our constructive suggestion, and I hope that's silenced some of our critics. Anyway, on with the blind, unreasoning rage.

Hugh   Yes, here we go. I've written a savage, angry, satire on jam jars that get separated from their lids.

Stephen	Now that is anger.

Hugh walks to piano. On top of the piano is a jar with no lid.

Hugh	*(Sings)* Where is the lid Where is the lid Where is the lid Where is the lid
	Where is the lid Where is the lid Where is the lid Where is the lid
	Does anyone know Does anyone know Does anyone know
	Where is the lid Where is the lid Where is the lid Where is the lid –

During this song Stephen has been saying:

Stephen	'Yes, it's over here.' 'Hugh! It's on the table.' 'Hugh, it's over here for God's sake.' etc.

Eventually Stephen can take it no more and attacks Hugh by beating him on the head with the jar or some similar heavyweight object.

Stephen looks down on Hugh's unconscious frame for a second.

We are devoting the rest of this programme to a tribute to the writer, comedian and light sketch actor, Hugh 'Excellent Sermon Vicar' Laurie, who died earlier today after a merciful accident that finally ended his long years of struggle with mental illness.

(Photo of Hugh appears.)

Stephen   *(Voice-over)* Hugh Laurie, whose real name was Hugh Laurie, was better known by his stage name: Hugh *Laurie*.

Cut to still of terraced house.

Hugh was born and brought up in a working-class home that his parents had specially built . . .

Pull back on still to reveal that the slum terraced house is actually set in rolling parkland in front of a beautiful stately home.

. . . in the grounds of their Gloucestershire estate. Like many shy children, Hugh learnt from an early age simply to blend in.

Cut to still of brick wall and lamp-post.

Caption   'Hugh Laurie, High Wycombe, 1967'

Stephen   His first acting job came in 1979, at Hereford Civic Centre, since renamed in Hugh's Honour, Hereford Civic and Amenities Centre.

Cut to interview with Rowan Atkinson.

Caption   'Nigel Havers'

Rowan   He was immensely dangerous. Such a dangerous actor. You always had this feeling when he was around that anything could happen. *(Pause)* Hugh Laurie, on the other hand, was about the dullest man I ever met.

Cut to interview with Nigel Havers.

Caption   'Paul Eddington'

Nigel   He brought to every one of his roles this quality of needing the money.

Cut to interview with bow-tied critic.

Caption   'Neil Hudd, TV and theatre critic for the *Daily Mail*'

Critic I'm so terribly clever, you see. That's one of the things I really admire about myself. I have this extraordinary ability to see, after the event, why something didn't work, and communicate it so wittily. I really am fabulous.

Cut to film of Stephen interviewing himself.

Stephen Stephen Fry, what is your fondest memory of working with Hugh Laurie?

Stephen The moment I knew he was really dead would be hard to beat.

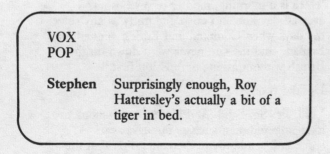

VOX
POP

Stephen Surprisingly enough, Roy Hattersley's actually a bit of a tiger in bed.

Jewellery

Hugh enters a jewellery shop. Stephen is polishing the back of his hand, for no particular reason, other than that it is screamingly funny.

Hugh   Er, good morning.

Stephen   Sir, it *is* a good morning. Sir is handsomely right to say so.

Hugh   Yes.

Stephen   Is sir aware, I am busy wondering, that I made so bold to remark on the goodness of the morning to the youngest of my mothers earlier today as she wheeled me into an upright position. Was sir in an awareness of that?

Hugh   No . . . no I had no idea.

Stephen   'Here is a morning, mother of my bosom,' I averred, 'as fine and crisp and gutty as any since the days when Compton and Edrich opened for England and the sun never went down on the British without asking permission first.'

Hugh   Ha, did you?

Stephen   I did, sir! Sir, I did. And if two broad-shouldered, long-fingered men such as ourselves can come independently to the conclusion that the morning they are currently experiencing is one of a goodness, then one of a goodness it must assuredly be.

Hugh   Really?

Stephen   Yes, sir, and you can spank me quietly with a chamois leather if it isn't so.

Hugh	Right, now . . .
Stephen	But sir hasn't come to trade insults on the state of the morning unless I am more vastly mistaken than a man who thinks Hilaire Belloc is still alive. Do sit down.

They both sit.

Hugh	No, I've . . .
Stephen	Sir has brought his handsomely sprung and finely wrought young body into this shop with the express purpose of going about the business of buying jewellery. Am I close to the mark?
Hugh	Absolutely.

Stephen stands.

Stephen	Do you mind if I stand, sir? I think perhaps this 'sitting down' idea of yours was a little ahead of its time.
Hugh	*(Also standing)* Right. Yes. The thing is I'm getting engaged and I'd . . .
Stephen	Would sir like an Opal Fruit?
Hugh	Um . . .
Stephen	A nice strawberry Opal Fruit? Or indeed any flavour?
Hugh	Thank you.
Stephen	*(Reaching for his hat)* I won't be long.
Hugh	Where are you going?
Stephen	There's a sweet-shop not half a mile up the road. I happen to know that they sell Opal Fruits.
Hugh	Well in that case, really don't bother.
Stephen	Don't bother?
Hugh	No, really.

Stephen	Is sir in absolute possession of sureness in this regard?
Hugh	Look. I really only came in here for jewellery, I thought if you happened to have an Opal Fruit on you . . .
Stephen	*(Feeling about on the top of his head)* 'On' me? Sir I have no Opal Fruit 'on' me. I can and will go further, I have never had an Opal Fruit on me. Eccentric, no doubt. Look, sir can search my head if sir is unconvinced.
Hugh	Look, forget the Opal Fruit. The Opal Fruit is irrelevant. I want an engagement ring. Can we concentrate on that?
Stephen	Sir, I am chastened and bowed. Ever the man of affairs, sir has reminded us all, all of our duty. An engagement ring for sir.
Hugh	That's right.
Stephen	What flavour of engagement ring had sir in mind?
Hugh	Flavour? What are you talking about?
Stephen	Just my little joke. You'll humour a dying man. We have a range of engagement rings that I would ask sir to cast over with sir's eyes, which I cannot help but notice are of a startling cobalt blue that would go very well with the wallpaper in one of my god-niece's back rooms.
Hugh	*(Leaving)* Right, that's it. I'm leaving.
	Stephen comes round with a range of engagement rings and blocks Hugh's egress.
Stephen	What about this one?
Hugh	What?
Stephen	What about this one?
Hugh	It's rather nice, I suppose.

Stephen	Sir, the issue of the rather niceness of this particular ring has been raised in Prime Minister's Question Time.
Hugh	How much is it?
Stephen	I would be wrong to let it go for more than forty thousand of your earth pounds.
Hugh	Forty thousand pounds!
Stephen	I would be equally at fault if I let it go for less than ninety.
Hugh	So it's between forty thousand pounds and ninety.
Stephen	Sir is as dogged in his pursuit of detail as Roy Walker, presenter of the never-popular show *Catchphrase* is dogged in his pursuit of a thick earlet.
Hugh	Perhaps you could, in preference to me walking out of here after hitting you very hard in the face, just tell me the frigging price.
Stephen	Since sir has been kind enough never to be Peter Sissons I can let sir have it for two hundred and eighteen poundingtons.
Hugh	£218?
Stephen	If you wish. And if sir will oblige me by promising never to wear green again I will throw this in for nothing.
	He brings out a velvet jewellery tray with a strawberry Opal Fruit as its centrepiece.
Hugh	An Opal Fruit.
Stephen	Yes, indeeding. A fruit of the genuine Opal persuasion. Perhaps sir will desist from ripping the kidneys from my nerveless frame if I offer him a taste to authenticate its strawberriness?
Hugh	No, no. I believe you.

99

Stephen   May I instead then, pausing only to pause . . .

                Pause.

                . . . congratulate you on your excellent taste?

Hugh   Thank you.

Stephen   Sir, I was talking to the Opal Fruit. Strawberrine but with a faint tang of small urine.

Hugh   Yes, yes. Quite so. Two hundred and eighteen pounds.

Stephen   Two hundred *and* eighteen pounds that should be.

Hugh   That's what I said.

Stephen   That's what *you* said. I barely spoke at all.

Hugh   Just put it in a presentation box if you would.

Stephen   No need. I'll wear it now.

Hugh   What?

Stephen   And I really think you should speak to my father now, darling. He's upstairs in the cellar.

Hugh   Right. I really am leaving, now.

Stephen   Leaving?

Hugh   Goodbye.

Stephen   But we're engaged!

                Hugh leaves. Stephen turns to camera.

                Men are such bastards.

Spies/Telescope

Stephen is looking out of his office window with a telescope. Hugh enters with a folder.

Hugh   Oh. Morning Control.

Stephen   Morning, Tony. I'll be with you in a minute.

Hugh   I say, that's rather a splendid device. Where did you get that, if you don't mind my prying into your affairs?

Stephen   I don't mind you prying at all, Tony. After all, you're only human.

Hugh   That's right, Control. I am.

Stephen   And what's more, you're a spy.

Hugh   That's true as well.

Stephen   Well to answer your question, Tony, you see it's my birthday today, and my sister Marie gave me this as a present.

Hugh   I didn't know you had a sister called Marie, Control.

Stephen   Marie isn't her real name of course, it's just a code name I've given her which prevents people from *discovering* her real name.

Hugh   Ah well, that's cleared up that little confusion.

Stephen   Her real name is Maria.

Hugh   Oh. So you decided to opt for a code name that was quite similar to her real name, then Control?

Stephen   Yes. It makes it much easier to remember.

Hugh   Huh. You are a wily old fox, Control.

Stephen	Anyway. This contraption is called a telescupe, Tony.
Hugh	A telescupe?
Stephen	Yes. Although I should point out that that's also a code name, in fact.
Hugh	Say no more, Control. Hush hush.
Stephen	Mmm. Although I don't think I'm speaking out of school if I tell you that this device enables one to see things very clearly over quite a long distance. Here, you can have a go yourself.
Hugh	Control, I really don't know what to say.

Hugh goes over to the telescope.

Stephen	Don't mention it, Tony. Now have a look at that man down there standing next to the telephone kiosk.

Hugh looks through.

Hugh	Gosh Control. You weren't exaggerating when you said it allowed you to see things very clearly. He could almost be in the room with us.
Stephen	That's very true, isn't it? But here's where the telescupe comes in. Because Tony?
Hugh	Yes?
Stephen	He isn't in the room with us.
Hugh	Well I thought he wasn't in the room with us Control, but it's nice to have it confirmed by you.
Stephen	He's actually on the other side of the street.
Hugh	Hmm. He appears to be looking this way, Control, with . . . wait a minute . . . yes, Control, that man is looking at us . . . with a telescupe.
Stephen	Yes, Tony. My theory is that he is an enemy agent charged with the task of keeping us under surveillance.

Hugh	What a confounded cheek, Control. I've a good mind to ring the police and have him moved on.
Stephen	Steady Tony. I've got a better plan.
	Stephen starts dialling.
	I got Valerie to find out the number of that telephone kiosk.
Hugh	Control, your plan is working. The man has picked up the receiver.
Stephen	*(Into telephone)* Hello? Enemy Agent? It's Control here. *(Pause)* Very well, thank you. Please stop keeping us under surveillance. Thank you.
Hugh	Yes, Control. He's going away.
Stephen	*(Wiping his hands)* There, Tony. Another small but significant victory for our side.
Hugh	Congratulations, Control.
Stephen	Now you go and fetch us a nice cup of coffee, and we'll pretend this whole ugly incident never happened.
Hugh	I can go one better than that, Control.
	Hugh exits and enters with a cup of coffee tied up in a red ribbon.
	Happy birthday to Control. Happy Birthday to Control. Happy Birthday to Control. Happy Birthday to Control.
Stephen	Oh get along with you.
Hugh	Aren't you going to open it?
Stephen	Boh!

Psychiatrist

Hugh enters a psychiatrist's surgery or studio, or office or whatever they call them.

Stephen Good morning, Mr Meddlicott is it?

Hugh Yes. You look a bit young to me. Still, I suppose you'll do.

Stephen Well, that's nice. Now, I shall call you Arthur, if I may.

Hugh You may not. You'll call me Mr Meddlicott.

Stephen raises his eyebrows.

And don't simper.

Stephen Very well. So why are you here, Mr Meddlicott?

Hugh Well, why do you think? You're a psychiatrist aren't you? I'm not here for dancing lessons or free sex, I've come to be cured.

Stephen Cured of what?

Hugh For heaven's sake man, do I have to teach you your job? Madness of course. I'm slightly mad and I'd like you to cure me. 'Of what?' Tt!

Stephen You're mad?

Hugh Yes! Am I going to have to repeat everything twice? Now I'm a busy man, so if you'll just get on with it, I'd be very grateful.

Stephen Would you like to tell me why you think you're mad?

Hugh Oh what is this, some sort of game? Do you imagine I've got time to waste *thinking* I'm mad?

104

	I *am* mad. Just take my word for it, will you, and let's have a little less lip.
Stephen	So how does this madness of yours manifest itself?
Hugh	At half past four every day I do something weird.
Stephen	Go on.
Hugh	Go on what. I'm waiting for half past four, aren't I?
Stephen	*(Looks at clock)* It's four thirty-three.
Hugh	I can see that. I'm running four minutes late today on account of your incessant yakking.
	Pause.
Stephen	*(Looks at clock)* Four thirty four.
Hugh	Right. For heaven's sake, watch closely.
	Hugh takes off his shoes, then removes a piece of bread from either jacket pocket and puts a piece in either shoe.
Stephen	You take off your shoes. And you put a piece of bread in each one.
Hugh	I know I do. What *is* your problem?
Stephen	Do you leave the bread there?
Hugh	Leave it there? Of course I don't leave it there. Are you some kind of idiot?
Stephen	Please go on. What happens next?
Hugh	I take the bread out of the shoes and hide it in my secretary's handbag. Then at four thirty-one, I take it out of her handbag and throw it in the bin.
Stephen	But you won't be doing that today, because your secretary's not there.
Hugh	Oh, give the man a bloody *medal.*
Stephen	So. *(Pause)* That's it, is it?

Hugh	Oh, I'm sorry, it's not enough for you. You'd rather I wrapped myself in bacon rind and pretended to be Florence Nightingale, would you? Well I'm sorry I'm as mad as I am. But no madder.
Stephen	Why do you think wrapping yourself in bacon rind would make you look like Florence Nightingale?
Hugh	Wh . . . I . . . are you an imbecile? I don't think anything of the kind.
Stephen	Florence Nightingale never wrapped herself in bacon rind.
Hugh	*(Angry and trying to explain)* I know she bloody didn't. BUT-IF-I-WAS-MADDER-THAN-I-AM-I-WOULDN'T-KNOW-WOULD-I-YOU-HALF-WIT.
Stephen	I see.
Hugh	So. What are you going to do about this madness of mine?
Stephen	Nothing. I don't think you're mad at all.
Hugh	You think it's perfectly usual to put bread in your shoes? On a daily basis. That's normal practice in your foul part of the world?
Stephen	You're welcome to a second opinion of course, but I don't think you're mad. Eccentric, certainly.
Hugh	And this is what we pay our psychiatrists for, is it? Well let me tell you, I shall write a very stiff letter to the *Daily Mail* about this. Now, cure me of my madness or I won't put my shoes on. Ever.
Stephen	*(Sharply)* You write letters to the *Daily Mail*?
Hugh	Not exclusively the *Daily Mail*. Sometimes the *Sun* or the *Mirror*.
Stephen	And they are published?

Hugh	Of course.

Stephen springs to his feet and goes over to his desk, picks up a copy of the Sun *or* Mirror.

Stephen	Is this one of yours? 'A good way to prevent your money being stolen is to . . .'

Hugh joins in.

Both	'Keep it in a special pocket sewn into your coat.'
Stephen	You're Mrs June Ellis of Stockport?
Hugh	Naturally.
Stephen	*(Reading from Mirror)* What about this . . . 'Why aren't –'
Hugh	'– bus conductors more friendly? A smile a day keeps the doctor away. And it's free too!'
Stephen	Chest size?
Hugh	Forty-two.
Stephen	Stay here. I'll get your strait-jacket.
Hugh	God the lengths you have to go to in this country to prove you're mad.

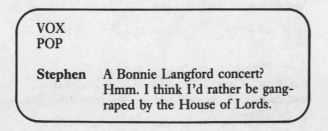

VOX
POP

Stephen	A Bonnie Langford concert? Hmm. I think I'd rather be gang-raped by the House of Lords.

Hard Man's Record

Close-up:

Car radio, hand on tuning knob.

Stephen's hand takes file out of briefcase.

Cut to outside of car. Stephen is putting briefcase on back seat of car. Hugh approaches car, opens door.

Hugh settles in his seat.

Stephen	Thank you for sparing the time for this.
Hugh	No problem.
Stephen	You admire Gary Davies?
Hugh	Don't get much time for that sort of thing.
Stephen	You should make time, Alan. A man should unwind. *(Stephen turns off radio)* Do you mind if I call you Alan?
Hugh	Fine by me.
Stephen	Good. Good. I just find Sally a bit awkward.
Hugh	I quite understand.
Stephen	Excellent. Now then Alan, I've got your record in front of me and it makes impressive reading. You've certainly knocked about the world a bit haven't you?
Hugh	Well, you know . . . I've knocked about the world a bit.
Stephen	Sorry. I meant to say 'you've done a lot of travelling'. You've done a lot of travelling, haven't you, Alan?
Hugh	Well, you know, I've knocked about the world a bit.

Stephen	Yes, you certainly have. But I'd like if I may to fill in one or two gaps, take a few side bearings, rough out some contours. OK with you?
Hugh	Fine.
Stephen	OK. '65, '66, you ran guns out of Macao using a refitted Dutch trawler.
Hugh	I can still smell those damn herring.
Stephen	'68 you popped up on the Ivory Coast smuggling refugees out of Nigeria. The following year there was that nasty caper with the Rhodesian mining company, and then in 1970 you became the reserve team coach for Oxford United. Correct?
Hugh	You've done your homework.
Stephen	But then, Alan, we seem to lose you. There's a gap, a hole, you appear to have vanished for four years. Four years is a long time in our business.
Hugh	You still haven't told me what that business is.
Stephen	Nor yet have I. A four year gap, Alan, until we find you cropping up again, this time in Indonesia, playing both ends against the middle in their civil war. From then on it's a series of apparently unrelated appearances, working with Uruguayan customs, a supply teacher in Maidstone, crop-spraying in Rawalpindi, Home Secretary in the last Labour government and then a short spell as Nigel Pargiter in the Archers.
Hugh	Someone had to do it.
Stephen	Oh yeah, sure.
Hugh	All right. Now it's my turn, okay? I've got to tell you I don't like being rung up by strange people I've never met before and having files read out at me. I don't like being asked questions by men in grey suits, yeah? Now why don't you tell me just exactly what is going on and who in blazes you are?

Stephen *(Chuckling at the file)* Oh it's all true. Insubordinate, impertinent, imprisoned twice for striking a senior officer, a rebel, a trouble-maker, a loner, an independent, a conniver, a misfit, a maverick, a trickster, an inveigler, a shyster, a shuffler, a shammer, an adventurer, a cozener, a thimblerigger, a pettifogger, a bilker . . .

Hugh Get to the point.

Stephen All right. We need a man, Alan. We need a man with exceptional abilities, a man with a record of success against all the odds, a man with the courage to try his hand at the impossible.

Hugh Go on.

Stephen We want you, if you can, to sit down and watch an entire episode of *The Krypton Factor*.

Hugh You're out of your mind.

Stephen Listen to me, Alan. It's never been done. No one has ever watched the programme from start to finish, and we desperately need someone to do it. Sure, we've all seen bits, but no one has ever gone the distance.

Hugh If I don't make it, you'll see that Judy's taken care of.

Stephen Of course, Alan, of course.

Hugh See you in hell.

Hugh gets out of the car.

Stephen What a man.

Borrowing A Fiver Off

Hugh   Good evening and welcome to *Trying To Borrow A Fiver Off*. Tonight I shall be Trying To Borrow A Fiver Off the conductor of the Bristol Philharmonic Orchestra, Neville Anderson. Good evening, Neville.

Stephen   Oh for heaven's sake, call me Neville.

Hugh   Ha, if you insist. Neville, can I borrow a fiver off you till Wednesday?

Stephen   Sorry, I've got nothing smaller than a twenty.

Hugh   Bye bye.

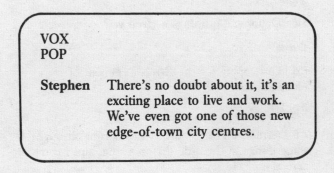

VOX
POP

Stephen   There's no doubt about it, it's an exciting place to live and work. We've even got one of those new edge-of-town city centres.

First Lines

Stephen addresses the camera.

Stephen   Ladies and gentlemen, all the sketches we've done on this show have been sort of finished, in one way or another. They start, they go along a bit, then they stop. More than one critic has drawn the parallel between our sketches and a nylon zip. But what we've never done on this show are the sketches that simply start – they start, with one line, sometimes quite a promising line, and then go nowhere at all. We'd like to show you some of them now, just so that you can get a glimpse of what might have been . . .

Cut to:

A traditional sketch shop. Stephen is behind the counter, Hugh enters frequently.

Hugh   Has Deborah Munnings arrived yet?

Cut to:

Hugh   I'd like to apply for the Royal Regiment of Homosexuals.

Cut to:

Stephen   Ah Dermot, there you are. I was sorting through some things in the attic this morning, and I came across your old legs . . .

Cut to:

Hugh   I'd like to open a Homosexual Bank account, please.

Cut to:

Stephen Your grandfather's a bit smelly, isn't he?

Hugh Yeah, well that's death for you.

Cut to:

Hugh *(Singing)* 'When somebody loves you, It's no good unless they love you'

Cut to:

Stephen Has Deborah Munnings arrived yet?

Cut to:

Hugh I'd like to apply to become a homosexual.

etc. . . .

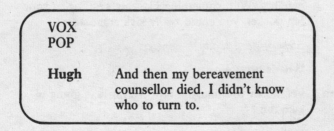

VOX
POP

Hugh   And then my bereavement
counsellor died. I didn't know
who to turn to.

Dammit 4

Stephen is sitting at a desk looking at a computer terminal. Hugh is leaning over his shoulder.

Stephen   Dammit, Peter.

Hugh   Thanks John.

Stephen   This is . . . what can I say? This is good work.

Hugh   Well I kind of hoped that we might be along the right lines here.

Stephen   Right lines? Dammit backwards into a narrow space, Peter, this is the best I've ever seen.

Hugh   Jill reckons ten days at the most. Which means we could have this up and running by the 29th.

Stephen   You mean . . .?

Hugh   Exactly, John. The Derwent Enterprises Board meeting. With something like this nestling in your hip pocket, you could really kick some arse.

Stephen starts to laugh smugly.

What's up, John?

Stephen   Peter, can you imagine how Marjorie is going to take this?

Hugh   Well John, at a guess I'd say that she'll be wilder than a hungry hellcat in a tornado.

Stephen   That's putting it mildly.

Hugh   Is it?

They both laugh creepily. The phone rings. Hugh picks it up.

Hugh	Hahaha. . . . Yes, hello? Hold on Sarah. *(To Stephen)* It's Marjorie.
Stephen	Haha. Well talk of the she-devil. Oh what the hell, I'll take the call.
Hugh	It's not a call, John. She's outside and she wants to see you.
Stephen	Marjorie's here?
Hugh	Yup.
	Stephen takes the phone.
Stephen	Show her in, Sarah.
Hugh	John, are you out of your goddamned mind?
Stephen	We don't know what it's about, Peter.
Hugh	To hell with what it's about, John! You and I have broken our arses building up this health club, with Marjorie gunning for us every centimetre of the way, and now you're going to let her swan in here . . .
Stephen	Now listen to me, Peter . . .
Hugh	Listen be damned! In case you'd forgotten, John, that bitchfiend tried to break us in two . . .
Stephen	Peter . . .
Hugh	I'm not going to let you do it, John!
	They are now nose to nose across the desk. In the background the door opens and Marjorie enters. She is late forties, Joan Collinsish glamour.
Marjorie	Hello John.
Stephen	Hello Marjorie.
Marjorie	Peter.

115

Hugh says nothing.

Marjorie   I hope I'm not interrupting anything?

Stephen   Not at all. Peter and I were just running over one or two things.

Marjorie   Are you all right, Peter? You seem a little uncomfortable.

Hugh   Yeah. Maybe I'll go outside and get a bite of air. The atmosphere in here seems to have got to my stomach.

Exit Hugh. Stephen and Marjorie look at each other for a while.

Stephen   You look well, Marjorie. You look damned well. New breasts?

Marjorie   Swiss.

Stephen   They suit you. I like what you've done to your hair. Looks much better there.

Marjorie   Thanks John, you look pretty fit yourself.

Stephen   Fit? Yeah, one of the perks of running a health and leisure business I guess. That is . . . if I still do run it?

Marjorie   The meeting will decide, John, you know that.

Stephen   *(Pouring two drinks)* And who will decide how the meeting goes, Marjorie? Dammit old man Ashby's in your pocket, Dexter and O'Neill will do whatever you damned well tell them and Tim will jump with the tide. Do you still like it straight up?

Marjorie   Two lumps of ice.

Hugh has appeared at the window and is looking jealously in.

I do whatever I do for the boy, John. You must know that.

Stephen   Yeah, the boy. Have you taught him to hate me, Marjorie?

Marjorie   Hate you? *Hate* you? You'll never really know me, will you.

Stephen   Not if I live to be a chairman.

Hugh is trying to listen.

Marjorie   Peter resents me.

Stephen   Peter? Dammit in top gear, Marjorie, what are you after?????

Hugh   *(Muffled, through the glass)* Yeah? What are you *after*??

They don't hear him.

Marjorie   I just want you to know, whatever happens after this meeting . . . that it wasn't personal, John. Strictly business. I still like you . . . a lot.

Stephen   *(Roughly yet somehow tenderly)* Come here, you . . . you Marjorie.

They kiss deeply and erotically.

Hugh is distraught the other side of the glass. He hammers on it.

Hugh   Leave him alone you bitch-cat! John don't listen to her. Damn you!

They part, panting.

Marjorie   I'll see you round the boardroom table.

Stephen   Yeah . . . round the boardroom table.

She makes to leave.

Oh and Marjorie . . .

Marjorie   Yes?

Stephen   Damn you to hell you're one hell of a woman.

Marjorie   I know. Well . . . you know where to find me.

Stephen takes an Oedipal decision.

Exit Marjorie.

Stephen   *(Following her)* Daaaaaamn!

Hugh climbs in through the window in a desperate bid to stop him. He trips over.

VOX
POP

Stephen   Chris Patten? Isn't he Margaret
Thatcher's new corporate logo?
I'm not sure.

Beauty and Ideas

Stephen is as we remember him from "Language Conversation". So is Hugh. But he's warier. He's done this before.

Stephen   So, in a sense, in a sense, in a *sense*, Duncan, we are left with those two. Two. None other. Nary another, not one other more. We have, on the one side of the divide, the gulf, the chasm, the DIVIDING LINE, if you please, we have the beauty of ideas, and on the other, the other side, oh, I don't know, the other *term of the equation* if that's nicer, we have the idea of beauty. Am I sensing through? Am I connecting?

Hugh glances at the camera in friendly fashion.

Hugh   We're busy discussing the beauty of ideas and the idea of beauty.

Stephen   Hold a thought for me, Geoffrey, I'll give you the thought, hold it for me. Would you please?

Hugh   I'm going to hold a thought, now.

Stephen   If beauty is only an idea, a form, a paradigm, a pattern, a template, an ideal, an idea, if you like, with an '1', then what is 'the beautiful'? Beauty is unattainable, but 'the beautiful' surrounds us. We return to language. Philip, we're back with language again. That's the thought you'd be ever so to splendid for me.

Hugh   We've made a return to language. That's the thought I'm holding.

Stephen   Listen to me lovelet, language circumscribes beauty, confines it, limns, delineates, colours and contains. Yet what is langage but a tool, a tool we

	use to dig up the beauty that we take as our only and absolute real?
Hugh	Language is a tool.
Stephen	So I'm finding myself with some surprise and no little alarm hurling a paradox at you. Beauty is our only reality and yet it is an ideal. It is the surface-tension of the membrane that stretches between us and the vision of beauty that language seeks to disperse, as a detergent might dissipate or dissolve a droplet of oil.
Hugh	I'm in trouble now.
Stephen	Hush, tish, vibble, I'm streaking ahead. Let me explain, expand, expound and exposit.
Hugh	Would you?
Stephen	I find you beautiful. But you are not beauty.
Hugh	Whoops.
Stephen	Therefore you contain a property of beauty. Therefore the substance of which you exhibit a property must exist. Where is it?

Hugh looks about helpfully, in case it is on the table or has been left on the floor.

	That is language's task. Who was it who said 'Language is the universal whore that I must make into a virgin?' Who was it?
Hugh	Kate Adie?
Stephen	I think it was Karl Kraus. But it needn't have been. Now. Tommy, time to ask you to give back the thought I bade you hold for me.
Hugh	I was holding the thought 'We've made a return to language.'
Stephen	Correctly correctington. Language pursues beauty, harries it, hounds it, courses it across the

roughlands of truth and enquiry AND IN SO DOING CAN BE BEAUTIFUL ITSELF. Ripple on ripple, image within image, a wheel within a wheel like the circles that you find in the windmills of your mind.

Hugh   Noel Harrison.

Stephen   Noel, as you so rightly, Harrison. Language can be beautiful. And Madeline asleep in lap of legends old. Plenitude. Dishes. Martita. Breasts. Tumble. Emolument. Forage. Smitten. Plenum. Vulva. Words that have their own sonority and beauty that is *ex*trinsic, *ex*trinsic to their connotational OR DENOTATIONAL referends.

Hugh   I think he said vulva.

Stephen   So Timothy I'll leave you with a thought, a breath, a fruit that drops from the boughs of my imaginings. Think beauty but be beautiful. Say beauty, but say it beautifully. Beauty is duty and duty beauty. So there. Goodnight. I don't feel quite so well now.

Hugh   *(To camera)* I'll talk to you later. B-bye.

VOX
POP

Hugh   The exciting thing about Chris Patten is that he's bold and imaginative.

Amputated Genitals

Stephen is coming groggily round in a hospital bed. Hugh as doctor, sympathetically gazes down.

Stephen   Oo-er.

Hugh   Mr Kerniff . . .

Stephen   Mmm.

Hugh   Mr Kerniff, how are you feeling?

Stephen   What happened?

Hugh   You probably don't remember Mr Kerniff, but you were in a very serious accident.

Stephen   A van.

Hugh   No. An accident. You were on your bicycle, and you were hit . . .

Stephen   By a van.

Hugh   That's it.

Stephen   Am I all right?

Hugh   You're going to be fine, Mr Kerniff. Lots of drink and plenty of hot sleep.

Stephen   Right.

Hugh   But I'm afraid you did sustain a very serious injury to your genitals.

Stephen   My genitals?

Hugh   *(Holds up stainless steel tray)* As you can see.

Stephen   Oh dear.

Hugh   Oh, as you rightly say, dear. We had no choice but to remove them.

Stephen	Oh no.
Hugh	Oh, as you didn't rightly say, yes.
Stephen	However will I manage?
Hugh	Hmm. Did you use them often, Mr Kerniff?
Stephen	Well, not really. But it was nice to know that they were there.
Hugh	Quite. Well all is not lost, Mr Kerniff. Medical science has advanced a great deal. Prosthetic and substitute legs, arms, even noses, are now commonplace.
Stephen	You supply substitute genitals?
Hugh	Say hello to Killer, Mr Kerniff.

Hugh leads on a nasty-looking Doberman.

Stephen	You're not going to . . . I mean, surely you can't. For heaven's sake, I don't want a dog's genitals!
Hugh	Oh what an almost amusing misunderstanding, Mr Kerniff. No no no. Killer will simply be your substitute for having genitals.
Stephen	I beg your pardon?
Hugh	Yes, I'm sure you've seen people walking round with Dobermans before?
Stephen	Well . . . yes.
Hugh	Yes, well for men who have no genitals, the ownership of a Doberman or similarly violent animal acts as an important psychological crutch. And I stress the word 'important'.
Stephen	Owning a Doberman is a substitute for having genitals?
Hugh	Indeed yes, Mr Kerniff. Thousands of people compensate for genital inadequacy by owning large dogs.

Stephen	But why?
Hugh	Beats me, Mr Kerniff. I'm only a doctor. In addition we will provide you with a diving watch, a year's subscription to *Guns & Ammo* and this combat jacket. And these are yours too.

Hugh drops a diving watch, a gun magazine, a combat jacket and a bunch of keys on Stephen's bed.

Stephen	Wh . . .?
Hugh	Keys to your rusty white van.
Stephen	But, Doctor . . .
Hugh	Yes, Mr Kerniff?
Stephen	I appreciate that you're trying to help here, but I also happen to use my genitals for, you know, getting rid of my urine . . .
Hugh	Oh don't worry, that's the beauty of the system. When people see you wearing a combat jacket and driving round in a white van with Killer, the piss will be taken out of you constantly.

VOX
POP

Stephen	I suppose in an ideal world I would be in bed with Philip Schofield right now.

Fast Talker

On a street somewhere. Stephen is trying to interview Hugh as the eyewitness to a road accident. Hugh is a fast-talking, over-eager Australian. Stephen has to keep stepping in and out of shot to restrain Hugh.

Stephen *(To cameraman)* Are we ready?

Hugh Yup. Any time. I was standing . . .

Stephen No, I was just talking to the cameraman.

Hugh Right. Got you.

Stephen OK. So basically I'll just ask you what you saw . . .

Hugh Well this guy came haring round the corner, must have been doing about fifty . . .

Stephen Wait a minute . . . Can you wait until . . .

Hugh Oh right.

Stephen I'll ask you a question about what you saw . . .

Hugh Yeah, this guy came round that corner, I thought he was going to hit that wall over there . . .

Stephen No. Can you wait until I've asked you the question . . .

Hugh Sorry. Sorry.

Stephen Now then . . .

Hugh This guy came round that corner there . . .

Stephen WAIT . . . a minute.

Hugh Sorry. I thought you . . .

Stephen No. Just wait. Brian, are you ready?

Brian	*(Off)* Ready.
Hugh	OK. This guy came haring round that corner ...
Stephen	Shut up!
Hugh	Oh yeah, right.
Stephen	Please do not say anything until I've asked you a question.
Hugh	Oh I get you. Right, sorry.
Stephen	Good. Now Mr Travis, I believe you ...
Hugh	Yeah that's right, and this guy came round that corner over there doing about fifty ...

Stephen goes right up to Hugh, noses almost touching, and screams at him.

Stephen	WAIT ... UNTIL ... I'VE ... ASKED YOU ... THE ... QUESTION!!

Longish pause.

Hugh	OK.
Stephen	Thank you ...
Hugh	This guy came ...

Stephen punches Hugh in the face incredibly hard.

VOX
POP

Stephen	*(Wine tasting)* Um ... the first one was dog the second cat. No? They were both cat?

Yellow Pages

Charming old man enters bookshop, where Hugh and Stephen serve.

Old Man   Good morning. Do you have a copy of *Fly Fishing* by J. R. Hartley?

Hugh   I knew it, I knew it.

Stephen   I said this morning.

Hugh   Would you believe it, we had a whole shopful of them, and now . . .

Camera pulls back to reveal an empty shop.

Old Man   Well, that's the power of advertising I suppose.

Hugh   Absolutely. Mind you . . .

Stephen   We do have 30,000 copies of *Yellow Pages*, can't shift 'em.

Old Man   Ooh. Can I order one?

Hugh   Well we've got them here.

Old Man   No, no. I have to order them you see.

Stephen   Well, yeah. All right then. We can order one for you.

Old Man   You can? That's marvellous. My name? Of course . . . it's Pages, L.O. Pages.

Hugh   I never asked him his name, did you?

Stephen   No.

Stephen   *(Voiceover)* Good old L.O. Pages.

Spies/Twin

Stephen is looking at a picture on the wall, dressed in a very unControllish sort of way. Painter's smock and multi-coloured scarf. Hugh comes in, and starts talking before he sees Stephen.

Hugh   Morning Control. Sorry to bother you with this but . . .

He sees Control and is slightly startled by his clothes.

I was wondering . . . whether . . .

Stephen   Morning.

Hugh   Morning. If you'll allow me to say so, Control, you appear to have radically changed your appearance and manner of dressing.

Stephen   Ah, we've got a little bit of a crossed line here, I'm afraid. I'm not actually Control.

Hugh   You're not Control?

Stephen   No.

Hugh   Well now I don't know whether I'm coming or going.

Stephen   Don't worry. I'm Control's twin brother. How do you do?

Hugh   Oh I see. How do you do? You really do look awfully like Control, you know.

Stephen   Yes, people have frequently remarked on the similarity between myself and Control, it's true.

Hugh   My name's Tony.

Stephen   My name's Control.

Hugh   Sorry?

Stephen	It's a bit confusing but you see my mother could never tell us apart right from the day we were born, so she decided to call us both by the same name. She called us both Control.
Hugh	You mean Control is Control's real name?
Stephen	That's right. Oh dear. Have I been indiscreet?
Hugh	Not at all. It's just that I always assumed that the name Control was just a cover for Control's real name, which was a closely guarded secret.
Stephen	Well, of course I've always known that his name was Control. Just as I've always known that my name was Control as well.
Hugh	You could knock me down with a feather.
Stephen	I expect I could if it was a large and heavy one.
Hugh	Yes. So. Do you happen to know where Control is?
Stephen	I'm right here, as it happens.
Hugh	Oh no! We're confused already!
Stephen	Oh, you mean my brother Control!
Hugh	Yes.
Stephen	He's presently painting an erotic mural somewhere in Earl's Court I should imagine.
Hugh	Oh dear. I may need a lie-down soon.
Stephen	Before you go to that extreme, Mr Murchison. I assume you are Tony Murchison by the way . . . ?
Hugh	I am. Though the way things are going perhaps I should say 'I think I am!'
Stephen	Yes. I like you already, Tony, if I may call you that.
Hugh	Please do.
Stephen	I was going to explain that I am something of the Black Sheep of our family. Control is a widely

	respected chief of the Secret Service and I am a not very respectable painter, though with a certain following in the louche areas of the metropolis.
Hugh	With you so far Control number two.
Stephen	And the thing of it is is that Control asked if I wouldn't mind changing places with him: me to run the Secret Service for a week, he to have a stab at painting an erotic mural in Earl's Court.
Hugh	Ah. I expect he's wanting to keep his undercover hand in.
Stephen	Very probably. So, Mr Murchison, have you got any secret documents you'd like me to sign?
Hugh	Well Control number two, I just need your permission to allocate funds for the purchase of that new safe house in Kensington that nobody knows the address of. Here are the estate agent's details.
Stephen	*(Looking through)* Oh, no Murchison. I can't possibly authorise our spending money on a house which has floral carpets and plain curtains.
Hugh	Ah.
Stephen	And look at the wallpaper in the hall. Far too busy.
Hugh	Right. I'll get to work on finding something more appropriate.
Stephen	Yes please.
Hugh	Meanwhile ... would a coffee be helpful at all?
Stephen	Well, I'd love a lemon tea if you can manage it.
Hugh	Well well well! Control?
Stephen	Yes?
Hugh	Even if I hadn't guessed earlier I'd know now that you aren't the real Control. Because Control?

Stephen   Yes?

Hugh   The real Control never has lemon tea. Always coffee.

Stephen   Voh!

Hugh   One lemon tea coming up, though.

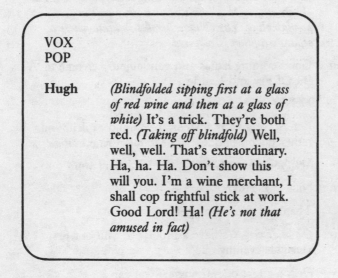

VOX
POP

Hugh   *(Blindfolded sipping first at a glass of red wine and then at a glass of white)* It's a trick. They're both red. *(Taking off blindfold)* Well, well, well. That's extraordinary. Ha, ha. Ha. Don't show this will you. I'm a wine merchant, I shall cop frightful stick at work. Good Lord! Ha! *(He's not that amused in fact)*

Swearing

Stephen and Hugh enter with their mouths gagged with tape, like anti-nuclear protesters (according to Hugh, who knows about these things).

Owing to the inaudibility of the irrepressible twosome, subtitles (But not subtleties, never subtleties).

Stephen	Mm . . . mmm . . . mmm mmm.
Hugh	Ng . . . ng . . . ng . . . ng . . .

It is understood that the following dialogue is subtitled. Where it says Hugh and Stephen they will in fact be mumbling. The obliques strokes indicate where a separate caption is required.

Stephen	Good evening ladies and gentlemen/welcome to 'A Bit Of Fry and Laurie'./
Hugh	Hello./
Stephen	Before we go any further, we should explain/ our rather unconventional appearance this evening./
Hugh	Yes, you normally sit on the left, don't you?/
Stephen	Nice gag, Hugh./
Hugh	Thanks, I made it myself./
Stephen	*(To audience)* We have a problem/ with our first item this evening . . ./
Hugh	Only a slight one, though./
Stephen	Yes, we've licked bigger problems than this / eh Hugh?/
Hugh	Yes, there was that very funny time when . . ./
Stephen	Oh shut up./

Hugh	Right./
Stephen	We are wearing these gags as a protest/
Hugh	Write on/
Stephen	Our first item tonight, my sweet little honeyclusters/ is a searing insight into real life,/ and perforce relies on using/ the language of the street./
Hugh	Swearwords . . ./
Stephen	Swearwords, exactly. But we have been banned from using actual swearwords/
Hugh	Bastards/
Stephen	So we have had to make up new ones /which are absolutely pitiless in their detail./

Hugh rips off his gag.

Hugh	And nobody can stop us from using them. Here they are . . .

Stephen rips off his gag. From now on, we are out loud.

'Cloff'.

Stephen	'Prunk' . . .
Hugh	'Shote' . . .
Stephen	'Cucking' . . .
Hugh	'Skank' . . .
Stephen	'Fusk' . . .
Hugh	'Pempslider' . . .
Stephen	No, we said we wouldn't use that one.
Hugh	Did we?
Stephen	Yes, that's going too far.
Hugh	What, 'pempslider'?

Stephen	Shut up.
Hugh	Sorry.
Stephen	And lastly, 'pim-hole'.
Hugh	Hah.
Stephen	So, here it is, ladies and gentlemen, our first sketch . . . and good luck . . .

Cut to 'Witness'

VOX
POP

Hugh	I'm afraid I was very much the traditionalist. I went down on one knee and dictated a proposal which my secretary faxed over straight away.

Witness

Stephen is a barrister. He is questioning Hugh, a police sergeant who is in the witness box. There is an elderly, fruity sort of Judge, Ralph, and a nasty-looking piece of work in the dock.

Stephen	Can you tell us, Sergeant Henderson, what the prisoner said to you when you made the arrest?
Hugh	If I may consult my notes, m'lud?
Judge	Certainly, certainly, certainly. By all means. Yes.
Hugh	I apprehended the accused and advised him of his rights. He replied 'Why don't you ram it up your pim-hole, you fusking cloff prunker.'

There is a sensation in the jury box. A woman screams and two men faint clean away. Judge purses his lips and makes a note.

Judge	'Why don't you ram it up your pim-hole you fusking . . .' er, cloth-blanket was it?

Another scream. The sound of a juryman being sick.

Stephen	Er, I believe it was . . . er . . .
Judge	*(Testily)* Yes, yes?
Stephen	Cloff-prunker m'lud.

Sharp intakes of breath all round.

Judge	*(Bemused)* I see. Forgive my ignorance Mr Clarkson, but what exactly *is* a 'cloff-prunker?'

Another sigh of horror. Stephen is mightily embarrassed.

Stephen	Well m'lud it's . . .

Judge	*(Impatiently)* Yes?
Stephen	It's ... hem ... an illicit practice whereby one person ... erm ...
Judge	Well?
Stephen	Whereby one person frangilates another's slimp, m'lud.
Judge	*(Staggered)* He does what?
Stephen	He or she gratifies the other person by ... smuctating them avially.
Judge	Good lord. How absolutely disgusting. Do people really do that sort of thing?
Stephen	I believe so, m'lud.
Judge	In which case I dare say there are probably magazines devoted to this practice?
Stephen	Very possibly, M'lud.
Judge	Are you planning to introduce any of these publications in evidence, Mr Clarkson?
Stephen	I hadn't thought it wholly necessary, M'Lud.
Judge	Hmm. Slapdash, Mr Clarkson. Slapdash. Well. Carry on, carry on.
Stephen	Thank you m'lud. Now Sergeant. After arresting the accused, I believe you questioned him at the station. You have a transcript of the interrogation?
Hugh	Yes, sir. I asked him if he could explain his whereabouts on the night in question. He replied 'I was in all night, wasn't I, you pempslider.'
Judge	Pempslider?
Stephen	A pempslider, M'Lud is ...
Judge	*(Irritated)* Yes thank you, Mr Clarkson, I am not entirely uneducated in these matters.

Stephen	I beg your pardon, M'Lud.
Judge	I did go to Winchester, you know.
Stephen	Quite so, m'lud. If you would continue, Sergeant. He called you a pempslider.
Hugh	That is correct. And then . . . then, he called me a . . . I wonder if I might have a glass of water, m'lud?
Judge	Certainly not. This isn't America.
Hugh	He said 'Skank off, you cloffing cuck, you're all a load of shote-bag fuskers, so prunk that up your prime-ministering pim-hole.'

Complete pandemonium from all save the Judge who looks at the accused sternly. A policeman behind him is clutching a handkerchief to his mouth and heaving. Accused looks smug.

Stephen	*(Whimpering faintly)* My God.
Judge	And what did you say to that, Sergeant?
Hugh	*(Consulting notes)* I told him to mind his fucking language, m'lud.
Judge	*(Approvingly)* I should think so too.

VOX
POP

Stephen   You see, it's a problem of
discipline. Young people know
nothing of service. They should
all be forced to do some time
in the army. There's muggings,
rapings, beatings, violence, cruelty
– fair enough, that's the army.
But at least it teaches you how
to serve.

Dancercises

Stephen pirouettes onto what is already becoming known as 'the area'.

Stephen Last year I was overweight, short of breath, flabby and – it grieves me to say it, however sexily I might contrive to do so – unhappy. Since then a friend introduced me to Dancercises. I won't tell you who the friend was, but if I drop the hint that it was a prominent quantity surveyor, I think you'll guess. He put me onto 'Dancercises' and I must say it was the finest thing he's done in his otherwise futile and meaningless life. The key to Dancercise is the rather ingenious coupling of the word 'Dance' to the word 'circumcise'. The great disadvantage with most forms of keep-fit is that they are uncomfortable, unnatural and can often throw too much strain on the important parts of your family. And, let's be utterly frank, they can look and sound peculiar and embarrassing if performed in public. Dancing, or more properly, Dance, is natural and expressive. Let's suppose I'm a prominent Quantity Surveyor and Hugh is Geoffrey Cavendish, a client. While I work, you can see that it is easy to fit in toning and strengthening movements.

Goes over to where Hugh is.

Morning Geoffrey.

Does a little dance.

Hugh Hello Dennis.

Stephen Got any quantities for me to survey this morning?

138

Hugh	I've got a quantity that I'd love for you to survey if you're not too busy, Dennis.
Stephen	*(Moving and jiving freely)* Yes. This quantity here?
Hugh	That's the fellow.
Stephen	*(Surveying it)* Well, that's got that quantity surveyed? Any others?
Hugh	That's all for today.
Stephen	Thanks, Geoffrey. You'll let me know?
Hugh	Oh, Dennis. If there are any other quantities I find and I want them surveyed, you'll be the first to know.

VOX
POP

Hugh	As I see it one American life is the same as two European lives, four Japanese lives, seventy African lives and three hundred Central American lives. At least that was at the close of business yesterday.

Trick or Treat

Stephen is in the area, finishing off polishing his desk with a duster and a can of Pledge.

Stephen It is our firm belief on 'A Bit Of Fry And Laurie', married to a passionate girl from Stockton-on-Tees, that there is a right way and a wrong way to do everything.

He is walking out across the central set now towards a doorway set.

So I and my 'partner in crime', Hugh Laurie. *(He finds this inordinately amusing)* My 'partner in crime'!!! No, I call him that, but that's not really what he is. We don't really commit crimes together of any kind. That's just a ghastly and unacceptable phrase that I like to use sometimes. So, anyway, I and my, as I say, 'partner in crime!' . . . *(Wipes eyes)* Honestly! . . . are now going to demonstrate the right way and the wrong way to treat a couple of young children who have come round on Hallowe'en a-trick or treating.

Hugh is waiting wearing something rather odd and looking very excited.

Hugh That's right!!! Now, we're going to play it like this. Firstly we're going to show you the Wrong Way, that's THE WRONG WAY, and then we're going to show you the Right Way. I'll say that again . . .

He doesn't.

Stephen Good. So all we need now is to wait for the doorbell to ring.

140

They wait.

Stephen   Nice carpet, Hugh. Tideyman's?

Hugh   Who else, if you'll pardon the pun.

Stephen   What pun?

Hugh   Oh, wasn't there one? Sorry.

Doorbell rings.

Ah, the door.

Stephen   We'll answer it, shall we?

Hugh   Sounds a hot suggestion to me.

They answer the door. Two children stand without, wearing Hallowe'en masks.

Child 1   Trick or treat, mister.

Hugh   Ah!

Stephen   Toh!

Hugh   Let me see, did we prepare a little bag of jelly beans out back?

Stephen   We most certainly did, I'll go fetch them.

Hugh is left alone with the children. He ruffles the hair of one of them.

Hugh   So. You fond of football, young shaver-snapper?

Child 2   Yeah.

Hugh   Do you fancy Arsenal this year?

Child 2   No way. I quite fancy my sister though.

Hugh   *(Disconcerted)* Ahmm . . . er . . .

Stephen   *(Coming through)* There we go.

He ruffles their hair.

Child 1	Ta.
Hugh	Bye now.

Stephen shuts the door and smiles.

That was the wrong way. THE WRONG WAY!! Now for the RIGHT WAY. I won't say that ever again. The Right Way, the RIGHT Way.

Stephen	Nice pun, Hugh. Tideyman's?
Hugh	Who else, if you'll pardon the carpet.
Stephen	What carpet?
Hugh	Oh, wasn't there one? Sorry.

Doorbell rings.

Ah, the hot suggestion.

Stephen	We'll answer it, shall we?
Hugh	Sounds like a door to me.

They answer the door: two children stand without, wearing Hallowe'en masks.

Child 1	Trick or treat, mister.
Hugh	What?
Stephen	WHAT did you say?
Child 1	Trick or treat.
Hugh	Trick or treat?
Stephen	Trick or treat?
Hugh	Come here.
Stephen	Both of you. NOW!!!

The children approach. A bit scared.

Hugh	*(Hurling child number one bodily out of the door)* This is England, not America.

142

Stephen	*(Doing the same to number two)* NOT AMERICA!! You understand?
	Both children have flown out of the door.
	You see? A right way, and a wrong way.
Hugh	We thank you.
Stephen	Limply.

VOX
POP

Hugh	*(With an electronic organiser)* Ask me anything, a telephone number, what time it is in Adelaide. Tell you what, I can tell you exactly what I'll be doing on the third of August 1997, say. Hang on *(Presses a few buttons)*. Nothing. See, it says. Nothing.

Breast Delivery

Stephen answers the door. Hugh is standing there in delivery man gear, with clipboard.

Hugh	Morning. Mrs Bennett?
Stephen	Pardon?
Hugh	Are you Mrs Bennett?
Stephen	No.
Hugh	No?
Stephen	No.
Hugh	Wait a minute. Wait a minute. Can you prove that?
Stephen	Prove what?
Hugh	I'm not being rude, it's just that for all I know you might be a conman answering doors and pretending not to be Mrs Bennett. Lot of that goes on.
Stephen	Well . . . will a Driving Licence do?
Hugh	Not really, no. You might have stolen it, you see. Anything else you can show me, to prove you're not Mrs Bennett?
Stephen	How about Mrs Bennett?
Hugh	Sorry, not with you.
Stephen	If I show you Mrs Bennett, would that prove I wasn't her?
Hugh	It's a start.
Stephen	Darling!
Hugh	Yes?

144

Stephen	No, I was calling my wife. I'm Mr Bennett.
Hugh	Oh.
Stephen	Darling!
Hugh	No, look, don't bother. If you're Mr Bennett, you can sign for them. Would you mind?
Stephen	Certainly. What are they?
Hugh	Some breasts.
Stephen	Pardon?
Hugh	Your wife ordered a quantity of breasts from us, and we promised we'd have them here by Wednesday.
Stephen	Today's Friday.
Hugh	We had a puncture.
Stephen	Wait a minute, what's she doing ordering breasts?
Hugh	Search me.
Stephen	I mean for heaven's sake she's already got some.
Hugh	Tscch. Women. Don't start me off. They're never happy, are they? Just sign there for me.
Stephen	'Breasts times three'. Three?
Hugh	Spare.
Stephen	I see. Well thanks very much.
Hugh	Aren't you going to check the box?
Stephen	Why?
Hugh	Well . . . make sure they're all right.
Stephen	I'm sure they're fine.
Hugh	Mmm. We do get a lot of mix-ups.
Stephen	All right, then . . . one, two, three. They look fine.

Hugh	Ermm . . .
Stephen	Yes?
Hugh	D'you mind if I have a look?
Stephen	I beg your pardon?
Hugh	Just to check.
Stephen	You want to look at my wife's breasts?
Hugh	Well . . .
Stephen	You are asking me if you can look at my wife's breasts?
Hugh	Just a peek.
Stephen	*(Showing the box)* Tssch. All right then.
Hugh	Phwor. Not bad are they?
Stephen	I suppose they're all right.
Hugh	All right? They're fantastic. You're a lucky feller.
Stephen	Mmm. Actually, I'm a leg man myself.
Hugh	Really?
Stephen	Yes.
Hugh	Funnily enough, I've got some legs in the back of the van if you're interested.
Stephen	Have you?
Hugh	Yeah. Make a nice surprise gift for your wife.
Stephen	No, I shouldn't really. She's up to her waist in legs as it is.
Hugh	They're a bit special.
Stephen	Are they?
Hugh	Definitely.

Spies/Firing

Stephen is at his desk. There is a knock at the door, and Hugh enters.

Hugh   Hello, Control.

Stephen   Tony. It's you.

Hugh   That's right. I understand from Valerie that you wanted reasonably strongly to see me.

Stephen   Valerie is by no means leading you up the garden path, Tony, because I do want to see you.

Hugh   I find Valerie's usually right in these little matters.

Stephen   Ng.

Hugh   Control?

Stephen   Yes, Tony?

Hugh   Did you want, I'm wondering, to speak to me as well, or was it just seeing me that was on your mind?

Stephen   Well now Tony, there was something I wanted to ask you, but it's a little bit tricky actually.

Hugh   Tricky?

Stephen   Yes, Tony. Have you ever been in the position where you've had to tell someone you like quite a lot that you've got to fire them from their job?

Hugh   No.

Stephen   Ah.

Hugh   That didn't turn out to be too tricky a thing to ask me, did it?

Stephen	Yes. Thing is, Tony, I haven't quite said the really tricky thing yet.
Hugh	Ah. Would it be the kind of thing that would go better with a good cup of coffee, Control?
Stephen	Perhaps a little later, Tony. I wouldn't want to be thought of as hiding behind that cup of coffee.
Hugh	That's just as well, Control, because the cup of coffee I had in mind was going to be quite small.
Stephen	Tell me Tony, have you, in your position as subsection chief of the East German and related satellites desk, noticed the way the wind is blowing on the other side of the curtain?
Hugh	It's been blowing in odd kinds of ways, hasn't it, Control?
Stephen	It has, Tony. Glasnost, perestroika and related phenomena have had their effect on the political map of Europe in no uncertain terms.
Hugh	Yes, Control. Only this morning, I had to ask Valerie if she wouldn't mind going out and buying some new political maps of Europe, as ours were really quite out of date.
Stephen	Yes, it's shaken all our lives up a bit, certainly. But Tony . . .
Hugh	Yes, Control?
Stephen	It's also meant that our masters in Whitehall have started wondering whether they need quite so many people involved in spying.
Hugh	I'm not sure I fully understand, Control.
Stephen	Well they take the view, Tony, that nowadays, with the Russians simply ringing us up and telling us most of their secrets, we don't need to spend such a lot of money on finding them out.

Hugh	That's an astute piece of political thinking by our masters in Whitehall, Control.
Stephen	Yes, Tony, it is.
Hugh	How about that coffee now, Control?
Stephen	No, Tony. Not yet. Anyway, what this is all leading up to, Tony, if you haven't already guessed, is that I'm going to have to fire you from your job.
Hugh	Control. I'm slightly at a loss for words.
Stephen	Please don't think, Tony, that I'm getting any enjoyment out of this situation. This is one of the hardest things I've ever had to do in all my years of running the Secret Service.
Hugh	Mmm. I certainly don't envy you, Control, having to pass on a bit of news like the one you've just passed on to me.
Stephen	Yes, it is very hard, Tony.
Hugh	Oh well, Control. I suppose that's that, then.
Stephen	Yes, Tony, I'm afraid it is. I really am very sorry.
Hugh	May I take this opportunity of saying how much I've enjoyed working for you, Control, and wish you the best of luck with all your future spying.
Stephen	Thank you Tony. I can honestly say that this place won't be the same without you.
Hugh	No, I suppose it will be a bit different because I won't be here.
Stephen	That's right.
Hugh	I'll be somewhere else.
Stephen	Yes.
Hugh	Well goodbye, Control.
	They shake hands.

Stephen   Goodbye, Murchison.

Hugh exits. Stephen sits down again and blows his nose. He picks up the phone.

Valerie? Could you bring me a cup of coffee? *(Pause)* How do I like it? I like it the way Tony Murchison used to make it.

VOX
POP

Stephen   If things had worked out differently it's strange to think *I* would now be Foreign Secretary and Douglas Hurd would be an assistant librarian. Weird, isn't it?

The Robert Robinsons

The Robert Robinsons each have behind them a word roller, like the one on Call My Bluff. *To start with it says 'the Robert Robinsons'. Each time they ting a bell which is on the table in front of them, the word roller goes round and a new word appears.*

Stephen   Ah, well now yes, good evening. That much is certain.

Hugh   Though tish ah, nay, hush and fourpence, Mr Dwyer.

Stephen   And an extra point for being so clever!

Hugh   Would that it were, would that it were.

Stephen   Ah, indeed, would that it were, Mr Charteris, would that it were.

They both ping their bells and the words 'pompous' and 'insufferable' appear.

Hugh   Here's a thing, not that pish and tish.

Stephen   I have a letter from a Colin Elgood of Carshalton Beeches telling me he turns his carrier bags inside out so as not to give free advertising to Mr Sainsbury and men of his ilk.

Hugh   Nay men of his stamp.

Stephen   Of his ilk, stamp and kidney.

Hugh   Your answer is better Mr Meredith, so much better but wrong, sadly wrong.

Stephen   And an extra mark for being clever!

They ping and the words 'self-satisfied' and 'fraudulent' appear.

Hugh	Ah, we have a plump! Someone has plumped. Go on, Mr Harris, have a plump too.
Stephen	Hish, tusk, ah now, it only remains for me to declare the Twee family winners of our little game.
Hugh	An extra mark followed by this round of applause.
	Ping! The words 'absurd' and 'gasbag' appear.
Stephen	Ah, the pity of it, the pity. Time, our old enemy, comes round again.
Hugh	Nish, tussock, flimp and fivepence.
Stephen	We bid you goodbye.
Hugh	We bid you farewell.
Stephen	But ah, though, flish, bish and trivvock, not for ever.
	Ping! The words 'sod' and 'off'

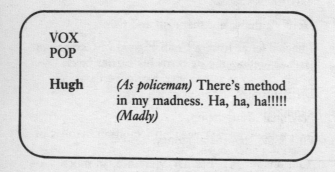

VOX
POP

Hugh   *(As policeman)* There's method in my madness. Ha, ha, ha!!!!!
(Madly)

Technophobia

Stephen   Did you . . . I don't know, you may have done
          . . . last night . . . see that Horizon . . . er . . .
          documentary, is it? Is that what they're called?

Hugh   Horizon documentary, yes, I think so. You mean,
          on the er . . .

Stephen   Television.

Hugh   Television, that's right.

Stephen   Yes, television. I think it's a . . . documentary. Did
          you see it?

Hugh   No, I didn't, I'm afraid. I was out last night.

Stephen   Oh dear, you didn't record it?

Hugh   Record it?

Stephen   Yes.

Hugh   Oh I see what you mean. No, we've got one of
          those er . . .

Stephen   Recording . . .

Hugh   Yes, those machines that record . . .

Stephen   Recording machines . . .

Hugh   Is that what they're . . .?

Stephen   I think so.

Hugh   Yes, well, we've got one, but I'm afraid neither of
          us knows how to work it.

Stephen   Oh how terribly amusing.

Hugh   It is, isn't it? Amusing and eccentric.

Stephen   Terribly.

Hugh   Yes I'm just hopeless with anything mechanical . . .

Stephen   Oh me too. My wife gave me an electric toothbrush last Christmas, and I just can't work it out at all . . .

Hugh   Oh how amusing and eccentric.

Stephen   Isn't it? Isn't it incredibly amusing and eccentric?

Hugh   I can't even work an ordinary toothbrush.

Stephen   Can't you?

Hugh   No, I keep putting the wrong end into my mouth, and the toothpaste up my nose . . . I'm hopeless.

Stephen   Me too.

Hugh   My wife looks at me with one of those looks of hers that seems to say er . . .

Stephen   How amusing and eccentric?

Hugh   Exactly.

Stephen   Yes, there's another one of those documentaries on tonight, apparently.

Hugh   Really? Oh well I might watch it, then. What time, do you know?

Stephen   Half past eight, I believe.

Hugh   Half past eight, yes, that's when the big hand is pointing . . .

Stephen   Oh don't ask me. I can't deal with these confounded watch things . . .

Hugh   No, neither can I. My daughter gave this to me, and I can't get the hang of it . . .

Stephen   No, I'm much too amusing and eccentric to . . . you know . . .

Hugh   Me too. Far too amusing and eccentric.

Stephen   But I think it's at half past eight. It should be in the paper, anyway.

Hugh	Newspapers? Haha. . . .
Stephen	Hahaha . . . me too.
Hugh	Never know which way to turn the blasted page.
Stephen	Get it upside down . . .
Hugh	All over the place . . .
Stephen	I always give the paper to our young son to read, he's the only one who can work the confounded thing.
Hugh	Honestly. We *are* amusing and eccentric aren't we?
Stephen	Yes.
	Bell rings.
Hugh	Hello!
Stephen	Best be in the House for that debate on the electricity privatisation.
Hugh	Absolutely . . .

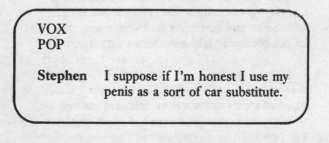

VOX
POP

Stephen   I suppose if I'm honest I use my
penis as a sort of car substitute.

A Vision of Britain

Stephen addresses camera. His hair is wild and peculiar. He stares through thick, black-rimmed spectacles.

Hugh is playing 'I vow to thee my country' throughout on the piano.

Stephen   Ladies and gentlemen, bear with me. Bear with me please. Don't stop bearing with me for a few moments. I have a vision, a vision of Britain. I see a country peopled by . . . a country peopled by people who, who . . . people it with charm, with grace, yes even with greatness. As they people it, they enhance it with their lightness, their amusing accents, their v-neck sweaters and their unusual children. This country shall be free and wide and pretty, and their people shall be free and wide and pretty. And there shall be villages and towns and family amusement theme heritage fun parks which shall smell of urine and vomit. And there shall be twelve water and sewage businesses and leisure dromes and huge edge-of-town crematoriums and day-glo bermuda shorts which are flecked with urine and vomit. I see 'Impact' as a new kind of flexible high-yield convenient cash and care card for the kind of person you are today and I hear the sound of many thousands of miles of motorways, conveniently filled with many hundreds of thousands of cars whose seats are stained with children and urine and vomit. And the interior of the cars shall be sweaty and hot and bad-tempered and the queue for the exit that leads to the family amusement heritage theme fun park shall be hundreds of miles long. And there shall be shiny

magazines out of which will fall many dozens
of smaller shiny magazines which shall offer
useful electronic golfing equipment and wall safes
disguised as three pin sockets and bright security
lamps and personal attack alarms and hand
freshen-up absorbent pads to soak up the urine
and the vomit. And the faces of the people who
are peopling this Britain shall be shiny and they
shall be flushed and pink for they shall know that
they are forging a new Britain of fun and heritage
and family leisure amusement and the boot of their
car shall easily accommodate the self-assembly fun
park that they shall erect in their bathrooms. As
yet, it is all only a vision, a vision of family heritage
urine and fun leisure amenity vomit. But soon,
soon, with luck, sincerity and steadfast voting it
may become a reality.

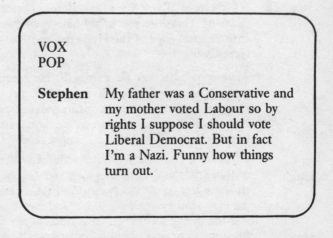

VOX
POP

Stephen   My father was a Conservative and
my mother voted Labour so by
rights I suppose I should vote
Liberal Democrat. But in fact
I'm a Nazi. Funny how things
turn out.

Ironic Self-Defence

Stephen   We live, don't we, in an increasingly age. Where once the village post office, a mug of Horlicks, Bing Crosby songs and a Kenneth More film were the only things the average Britain had to fear, nowadays every alleyway can conceal a threat, every encounter a violent confrontation, every telephone call an erotic nightmare. Arnold.

Hugh   That's right. It has become increasingly and abundantly that unscrupulous people have traded on the fear that now stalks the streets. Open any local newspaper or give-away sheet and you can read advertisements for self-defence classes in hai-ki-doh, ken-doh, play-doh, judo and a whole stain of martial arts. But people who answer the threat of violence with real violence of their own often find that it is *they* who end up in court, not their assailants. Nerelle.

Stephen   That's right. If you live in the Boroughbridge area of North Yorkshire you might have read this article in your local copy of the Helperby and Cundall *Advertiser.*

Voice-over: 'Discover Dr Patrick Fisher's amazing new key to non-violent self-defence. Repel muggers, rapists, attackers, insurance-salesmen, burglars, Christians and house-breakers without harm or fear of prosecution. Simply send £3.00 for *Fisher's Guide To Non-Physical Violence.*' Dwoyne.

Hugh   Thanks. Well, we're never one to resist a challenge so we duly sent off for Dr Fisher's book. Fwith.

Stephen   That's right. Moylinda.

Hugh   The 'book' turned out to be this. *(Holds up flimsy pamphlet)* The secret method that Dr Fisher

158

recommends? Well, it seems that there are two basic approaches.

Hugh & Stephen read them alternately, starting with Stephen.

Stephen   '1. The Flirty Come-on.'

Hugh   '2. The Disorientating Remark.' Testina.

Stephen   Thanks. So we decided to try this method out for ourselves. F-f-f-f.

Hugh   Yes indeed. We went out into Chichester's notorious East Gate and waited for the inevitable assault.

Caption   '1. The Flirty Come-on.'

Hugh is loitering on a bench, an expensive-looking briefcase on his lap. He is counting the money in his wallet.

A mugger sidles up next to him and whips out a knife.

Mugger   *(Waving it under his nose)* You know what this is?

Hugh   Yes. I do actually. Sweet of you to try and help me out, but I do actually know what it is.

Mugger   Right. Wallet.

Hugh   Wall . . . oh for heaven's sake you're mugging me.

Mugger   That's right.

Hugh   Oh, now you've . . . oh. Of all the people here . . . you've picked on little old me. I don't know what to say. I think I'm going to cry.

Mugger   Wallet.

Hugh   Of course, of course. Hold on, I'll just take the money and things out first, otherwise you'll have to

	lug them around all day, and there'll be no room for your own stuff.
Mugger	Look, get a move on.
Hugh	Oh sorry, of course. You've got things to do, of course you have, and here's me nattering away twelve to the dozen.
Mugger	Oh forget it.
Caption	'2. The Disorientating Remark.'
	Stephen is in an alleyway, he bends down to tie his shoe-laces. A man comes up from behind.
Man	Right. Do as I say and you won't get hurt. Lie down in that corner and drop 'em.
Stephen	I had an Uncle Geoffrey that looked just like you. He wasn't so old then and tasted slightly wider.
Man	Did you hear what I just said?
Stephen	I've got a note from matron you know.
Man	What?
Stephen	Unless you go away from here and leave me alone completely I'll write a poem in Lebanese and send it straight to Gary Lineker's doctor.
Man	Just get down in that corner.
Stephen	*(Shouting)* My name is an anagram of the Metropolitan Police and unless you stay here and do exactly as you tell me your breasts will become the property of Gerald Kaufman.
Man	*(Pushing Stephen to the floor and unbuckling his belt)* I said GET DOWN!
Stephen	Right-o. Fair enough. I should just mention though, that you can't fit quicker than a Kwikfit Fitter.
	Back to studio.

Stephen   So. A warning there. If Dr Fisher's Advertisement should find its way into your High Street Give-Away Market Trading Advertiser Sheet our advice is Trish.

Hugh   That's right. And remember. Dermidge.

Stephen   So, until. It's.

Hugh   Bye.

VOX
POP

Stephen   Well I was given one of those personal organisers, so when I went into work everyone said 'You're a bit of a yuppie!!!' It was so funny. Because yuppies are those new people you know who are very trendy. 'A bit of a yuppie!' Dear oh dear. That's probably the funniest thing that's ever happened to me.

The Cause

Hugh and Stephen are in a London club sort of place.

Stephen   Freddy.

Hugh   Oh, good heavens, Jack, I didn't see you there.

Stephen   Good evening, Freddy.

Hugh   Well, good evening, Jack.

Stephen   Now then, Freddy you're a decent sort of chap.

Hugh   Well, I, yes, I think so Jack, yes, I try to be a decent sort of chap, yes.

Stephen   Mmmm. Can I ask you a question, Freddy?

Hugh   Ask away, ask-a-bloody-way.

Stephen   Are you one of us?

Hugh   Am I one of us?

Stephen   Yes.

Hugh   Am I one of us?

Stephen   Yes.

Hugh   Not entirely sure I understand your question, Jack.

Stephen   Let me put it another way.

Hugh   Oh, would you Jack, yes, well, I'd be enormously grateful.

Stephen   Do you believe in the cause?

Hugh   The cause ...

Stephen   The Cause of Freedom.

Hugh   Well, Jack I suppose, generally, yes, yes, I do. If anyone's passing the hat round for freedom, I'll bung in a quid or two, Jack, yes.

162

Stephen	I thought so, I thought so from the first.
Hugh	Yes, I'm one of us Jack, if you want to put it that way.
Stephen	Excellent.
Hugh	Phew, well, we got there in the end, Jack, sorted that one out.
Stephen	It gets a bit more complicated now.
Hugh	Oh, Lord.
Stephen	Would you be prepared to do something in the cause of freedom?
Hugh	What sort of thing, Jack? Jumble sale, hand out leaflets? What?
Stephen	Put a bomb in a restaurant.
Hugh	Put a bomb in a restaurant. Ah Crikey. And leave it there, you mean?
Stephen	Leave it there. That's right.
Hugh	Yes, yes. You don't mean put it there, have a spot of lunch and then take it out again?
Stephen	No, I mean leave it there.
Hugh	Um, until it goes off?
Stephen	Precisely. Do you think you could manage that in the cause of freedom?
Hugh	Oh, Jack, Jack, I wonder if you wouldn't mind, sort of, joining up the dots for me, if you like.
Stephen	If it'll make it easier for you.
Hugh	I think it will, Jack, I think it will, because unless I've fainted and missed a whole chunk of the conversation, um, we've been sitting here, you

and I, having a nice old chat, putting the world to rights and so on, and then suddenly you're asking me to put a bomb in a restaurant.

Stephen   That's right.

Hugh   Those are the two dots I'd like you to join up, Jack. The nice chat and the bomb in the restaurant. Join them up for me, there's a good fellow.

Stephen   All right then, Freddy. There are certain people who do not believe in the cause.

Hugh   Don't believe in freedom, you mean?

Stephen   That's right.

Hugh   Oh, utter swines, and they eat in a particular restaurant, do they Jack?

Stephen   Some of them will be eating in a particular restaurant on a particular day.

Hugh   Ah, well, Jack, sorry to stop you, but, I've an idea, um, well, you know who these people are, Jack.

Stephen   Yes.

Hugh   And you know which restaurant they'll be in?

Stephen   Yes.

Hugh   Right, well, so here's the idea. We go in there, you and I, Jack and we sit down at their table and we hammer it out with them face to face. What do you say?

Stephen   Fight them, you mean?

Hugh   No, no, no, Jack, no: argument. You're a persuasive fellow, Jack – I bet we could sit down at their table over the soup, and you could talk and I'll back you to the hilt and I bet you anything we could have them believing in freedom by the time the pudding arrives. What do you say Jack?

Stephen	I don't think that'll quite do.
Hugh	It won't quite do. Well, all right Jack. How about this *(Laughs)* we pretend to put a bomb in the restaurant.
Stephen	Freddy . . .
Hugh	Yes, Jack?
Stephen	I think perhaps . . .
Hugh	Yes.
Stephen	I think perhaps that I was wrong about you.
Hugh	No, Jack, no. No you were absolutely right, Jack. Right as bloody rain, you were.
Stephen	Well, then.
Hugh	Well, Jack, it's just . . . I'm just the most awful duffer at this sort of thing.
Stephen	The restaurant is called the Étoile d'Or in Maddox Street. I suggest you put it behind the lavatory cistern. But it's up to you.
Hugh	Oh, Hell.
	Stephen (Gordon) and Hugh (Stuart) are at a restaurant with their wives.
Hugh	They've got a bigger table than we have.
Girl 1	Come on Stuart, this is fine.
Hugh	Look, there are two of them and they've got a bigger table. There are four of us and look at this. *(Bangs table)*
Girl 2	Oh Stuart for heaven's sake, a table's a table!
Stephen	Darling . . .
Hugh	Well, Jill, there we differ. To me there are tables and there are tables. Am I right Gordon?

Stephen	Well you know me, Stuart, table is as table does.
Girl 1	At least it's snug, poppet.
Hugh	What it is, poppet, is cramped. You should've used my name when you booked.
Girl 1	Well I did.
Stephen	What, Mr Poppet?

(They all laugh at Hugh)

(Hugh enters the restaurant as the character from the club, clutching briefcase with bomb in it)

Waiter	Good evening, sir.
Hugh	Good evening. A table for bomb please.
Waiter	Excuse me?
Hugh	*(Laughing hysterically)* A table for one. Sorry . . . bit nervous. I've never actually eaten a meal before.
Waiter	Well, you have chosen the perfect place to start. Follow me please.

(Cut back to Gordon and Stuart)

Stephen	So what did we think of the show?
Girl 1	Loved it. Thought it was really nice.
Stephen	Me too. High quality entertainment.
Hugh	I'm going to come right out and say it. To me, Jeffrey Archer is the finest playwright this country's turned out since William Shakespeare.
Stephen	That's a hell of a statement, Stu.
Hugh	Well let me go one further, Gordon. To me, Jeffrey Archer delivers.
Stephen	Oh the guy can write, no question.
Girl 2	Delivers, does he?
Hugh	I beg your pardon, Jill?

166

Stephen	Come on darling, you know what he means.
Hugh	No, it's all right thank you, Gordon. I can fight my own battles. What he delivers, Jill, to my mind, is quality drama . . . OK it's a little dangerous . . . OK it's not something that your average Joe punter is going to find all that accessible, but in the market he's working to he delivers and Gordon will tell you that's a compliment I use very sparingly indeed.
Stephen	It's true actually Jill, it's true. Stuart is not the kind of man to bandy the word 'deliver' around the place.
Hugh	Thank you Gordon.
Girl 1	Thought the sets were marvellous. They were really clever. Weren't they poppet?
Hugh	Yes, and the costumes were fantastic.
Girl 2	Sorry, they were wearing suits weren't they?
Hugh	Well, this is where Jeffrey Archer is so strong you see . . . in his observation. He's observed that in an office a large number of people wear suits. Isn't that right, Gordon?
Stephen	Absolutely, Stu.
Hugh	Well, he's observed that, you see. I mean the guy's got an eye for detail like well, there's no one like him in my book.
Stephen	To be fair to myself, Stu, I'd observed that people in offices wear suits too.
Hugh	No, no, no you hadn't, Gordon. You can only say that after you've seen the play. If I'd asked you before the play what people wear in offices you wouldn't have had a clue.
Stephen	I think I would've said suits.
Hugh	No you wouldn't, Gordon.

167

Stephen	I think I would.

(Hugh clicks his fingers at the waiter)

Hugh	No you wouldn't. Now wait a minute, look, that bloke came in after us and they're taking his order.

(Hugh is the character with the bomb, still clutching the briefcase)

Waiter	What would you like, sir?
Hugh	Crikey, yes.
Waiter	Something the matter, sir?
Hugh	Well, how many lavatories have you got here?
Waiter	Just one, sir, over there.
Hugh	Yes, I've tried that one, it's no good. No bloody good. It's the cistern, it's too close to the wall . . . you can't get anything between the cistern and the wall. Oh hell.
Waiter	Are you ready to order, sir?
Hugh	Order yes, well, to be perfectly honest I'm not awfully hungry.
Waiter	Well may I recommend a salad? Perhaps a smoked chicken salad? It makes a perfect light meal.
Hugh	Yes that sounds awfully good. Tell you what though, instead of that I think I'll just have a glass of water.
Waiter	Just a glass of water, sir?
Hugh	Lord no, make it a bottle. Or tell you what, half a dozen bottles. I mean you only live once don't you.
Waiter	Very good, sir.
Hugh	Oh hell.

(Stephen is a waiter. He goes to a table where a man sits alone)

168

Stephen	Good evening, sir.
Man	Good evening. I'd like to order some soup to start.
Stephen	Wait a minute, good Lord, you're Keith Bennett aren't you? The government minister?
Man	Well, as a matter of fact I am.
Stephen	I thought so, I knew it. Oh Mr Bennett, this is wonderful. I have to say I'm a great admirer of you and your policies.
Man	Really?
Stephen	Definitely. Can I recommend the halibut by the way. It comes with a nice black butter sauce.
Man	Thank you.
Stephen	You steered that broadcasting bill through the House of Commons didn't you?
Man	I did indeed.
Stephen	Brilliant, quite brilliant.
Man	Well I must say this is really most gratifying. So you really do admire my policies?
Stephen	Yes well, most people don't like you then?
Man	Well, you know how it is, we aren't always the most popular of people, we politicians.
Stephen	Yes, you must get used to people calling you a complete dickhead I suppose.
Man	No, not exactly.
Stephen	That speech you made about deregulating broadcasting . . . oh, I cheered for you that night. We must strive to offer the consumer a far greater range of choice, for too long broadcasting has been in the grip of a small élite. We must expand and offer more choice.

Man	Good heavens, you've remembered it word for word.
Stephen	Well, it was masterly stuff . . . oh my God, your cutlery . . . a silver knife and fork, I can't believe it. *(Removes cutlery)*
Man	Those are rather nice. They're not dirty are they?
Stephen	That this should happen to you of all people. I'm so sorry, I'll be right back.
Man	But they were fine . . .
	(Cut back to Gordon and Stuart)
Girl 1	Of course, Moulinex. All the way through I was trying to think where I'd seen that actress before. She's the one in the Moulinex advert.
Stephen	Oh that's right, the one about the blender.
Hugh	What, the wife?
Girl 1	Sorry?
Hugh	The actress who plays the wife? She's in some sort of advert at the moment, is she? Hello! Laura, wake up! The actress in the play who was playing the wife that we just saw tonight – you're saying she's in an advert at the moment?
Girl 1	The wife . . .
Stephen	Actually she was playing his daughter.
Hugh	Hold on, I'm probably getting her confused with someone, wait a minute . . . *(Looks at programme)*
Girl 2	There was only one woman in the play, Stuart.
Girl 1	And she was his daughter, Poppet.
Stephen	That was sort of the idea of the entire evening.
Hugh	Yes, daughter. What did I say?
Stephen	You said wife.

Hugh	Did I? This table is definitely smaller you know ... I mean all those other ones ...
Stephen	Look, that man over there, he's in the government. Isn't he a cabinet minister or something?
Girl 1	Keith Bennett.
Hugh	Got it! Roy Hattersley, you're quite right, Gordon.

(Stephen as waiter)

Stephen	I do apologise.
Man	Apologise for what? The fork and knife were fine.
Stephen	Oh it's very kind of you, sir, but I absolutely insist ...

(Pours bag of plastic coffee stirrers into man's lap)

Man	What's this?
Stephen	Your cutlery, sir.
Man	But these are plastic coffee stirrers.
Stephen	Yes I know, but at least you've got the choice now. I mean they may be complete crap but you've got the choice ... that's what's important, the choice ... *(Starting to shout and to strangle man)*

(Cut back to Gordon and Stuart)

Girl 2	That politician man's being strangled by a waiter.
Hugh	At least he's got a decent size table.
Stephen	Anyway to return to the play I have to say that although the acting was really good ...
Girl 1	Marvellous acting.
Stephen	I do think the play would've benefited from having a Paul Eddington in it.
Girl 2	*A* Paul Eddington?
Stephen	Well ideally, *the* Paul Eddington.

Girl 1	Isn't he wonderful?
Hugh	Well you see the thing about Paul Eddington of course is his timing.
Stephen	His timing is just so . . .
Hugh	Well it's the timing of a master.
Stephen	A friend of mine's sister married Paul Eddington's doctor.
Hugh	You never told me that, Gordon.
Stephen	Well, you know, one doesn't like to boast. Apparently it's well known that Paul Eddington has the second best timing in the business, after Nigel Havers.
Girl 2	What is timing, exactly?
Hugh	Well, it's a bit difficult to explain to a woman, Jill, but timing is basically the magic ingredient that Paul Eddington's got.

(Paul Eddington comes in)

Girl 1	What *is* it?
Paul Eddington	Yes, I'd like to know that too, I must say.
Stephen	I know your doctor's brother-in-law.
Paul Eddington	How nice.
Hugh	We were just explaining to our wives that you've got about the best timing in showbusiness.
Paul Eddington	After Nigel Havers.
Hugh	Level with us, Paul, would you class your timing as good, very good, extremely good or immaculate?
Paul	Well . . .

172

(Cut back to Hugh as the character with the bomb)

Hugh Hello, look, excuse me everyone, sorry to bother you and all that sort of filth . . . nearly forgot, long live freedom . . . the thing is there's a bomb . . . yes I know, rotten isn't it . . . the thing is it *is* about to go off so you might like to leave.

(Everyone runs out)

That's right, this way. Crikey, my bill!

(Bomb explodes)

Cut to 'Where Eagles Dare'

VOX
POP

Stephen It was just so funny. It was just so bloody funny. I literally died. It was bloody brilliant actually. No seriously, it was really funny, actually.

Where Eagles Dare

Hugh   You know that scene in *Where Eagles Dare?*

Stephen   Which scene?

Hugh   The one where Richard Burton is pretending to be a German agent.

Stephen   Oh yes.

Hugh   And in fact he's trying to find out the names of all the German agents in Britain. You know the one?

Stephen   Yes, yes. I remember it.

Hugh   Yes. That happened to me once.

Stephen   Did it, did it?

Hugh   Yes. In spades. In fact it's always happening to me. Lots of things from films happen to me.

Stephen   Is that right?

Hugh   You know that scene in *War Games* where the scientist calls the air-force general a pig-eyed sack of shit. Someone called me that the other day.

Stephen   The *other* day?

Hugh   Oh no, you're right. It was the same day. And *Fatal Attraction* could have been written about me. I almost sued when I saw it.

Stephen   You were persecuted by a one-night stand were you?

Hugh   No. No. I once went to bed with Glenn Close though.

Stephen   That's ridiculous.

Hugh   You're right, it's completely ridiculous. I went to bed with Michael Douglas.

Stephen   You went to bed with Michael Douglas.

Hugh   In a sense.

Stephen   What sense?

Hugh   A completely made-up untrue sense.

Stephen   Well as it happens, I've been to bed with Michael Douglas in that sense.

Hugh   Really?

Stephen   Well, snogged with him.

Hugh   How was it?

Stephen   I don't know. I made it up. But I'll tell you a really true thing that definitely happened to me, Kathleen Turner and Adrian Moorhouse. We were all lying in bed when . . .

Enter Paul Eddington very suddenly.

Paul   Immaculate, I'd say.

VOX
POP

Hugh   I had this idea for a television series, which I sent to Channel 4, in which every week people have to kill Noel Edmonds in a different way. But they said they were already working on something very similar.

Dammit Lavatories

Hugh is Peter, a lavatory attendant, inside a lavatory, making strange noises as he wrestles with some recalcitrant object or other.

Hugh   *(Off)* Come on. Come on . . . Gotcha.

Lavatory flush sound.

Stephen, as John, another attendant, crashes in and throws his coat onto a hook 'baa-ing'.

(Off) That you, John?

Stephen Who else, Peter?

Hugh   I was beginning to wonder where the hell . . .

Stephen Traffic, Peter, plain and simple.

Hugh   That's a bitch, John.

Stephen Took the switchback routes wherever I could, but the A47 is a car-park at the moment.

Hugh comes out of the stall carrying a plunger and wearing rubber gloves.

Hugh   Damn that ballcock.

Stephen It's no good blaming the cistern, Peter. So fill me in. How's business this a.m.?

Hugh   Quiet, John. Very quiet. Couple of noisy ones in stall three earlier on.

Stephen Really?

Hugh   Yeah, but mostly it's been quiet.

Stephen Right. Calls?

Hugh	Yeah, had one from the maintenance boys about fixing the towel rollers ...
Stephen	And?
Hugh	Can't make it till next Tuesday.
Stephen	Dammit.
Hugh	That's what I said, John.
Stephen	Damn, blast, triple damn, with an extra side order of damn.
Hugh	Yup. I said that as well.
Stephen	How the hell do they expect us to run a public lavatory complex without maintenance back-up?
Hugh	Beats me, John. They said they'd give it top priority ...
Stephen	Top priority my arse! *(Scrunches up a cup)* That's just a lot of hot air, Peter.
Hugh	I know John.
Stephen	Our clients can't dry their hands with hot air.
Hugh	Well actually ...
Stephen	Peter, don't start on this electric hand-drier stuff again. I've read your report, and it's good work, but now is not the time.
Hugh	Not the time? I wonder if you'd have said that when we were running the health club?
Stephen	Forget the health club, Peter, God damn it! Marjorie won. Pure and simple. It wasn't a clean fight I grant you, but she won. That's it. Over.
Hugh	You don't have to throw Marjorie in my face, John.
Stephen	I'm sorry, Peter. But dammit we've got a chance here, a chance to build the finest damned personal relief centre Uttoxeter has ever known.

177

Hugh	But when, John? What's the timeframe?
Stephen	Hell, Peter, only a fool would try and answer that question. Six months, maybe.
Hugh	Every morning when I leave the house, Sarah kisses me on the cheek ...
Stephen	Sarah? But your wife is Nancy?
Hugh	Sarah's the au pair, John. Helps out with a lot of Nancy's chores.
Stephen	Right.
Hugh	She kisses me and dammit if there aren't tears in her eyes.
Stephen	Peter, I know it's hard ...
Hugh	Kids have a hard time at school. 'Haha, Sherman's dad is a lavatory attendant ...'
Stephen	Don't ever say that, Peter. *(Scrunches up a cup)* The Peter I know is an equal partner in an enterprise that is going to alter the face of Uttoxeter's sanitation for ever.
Hugh	But the shame, Peter ...
Stephen	Peter, you're doing this for Nancy and the kids. When you refill the soap dispensers, it's for them. When you pick the cigarette ends out of the urinal, it's for them. When you unclog a U-bend with your bare hands, you're doing it for them!
Hugh	Dammit, John, you're right.
Stephen	That's more like it. *(Scrunches a full cup. It hurts.)* Now let's get to it.
Hugh	Shoot.
Stephen	Paper in every stall?
Hugh	Check.

178

Stephen	Evacuation points cleaned?
Hugh	Check.
Stephen	Even under the rim?
Hugh	Even under the rim.
Stephen	Mirrors polished?
Hugh	Till you could see your face in them.
Stephen	Good work.
Hugh	Had to close the urinal momentarily for cleaning purposes. And when something like that happens, as you know, the weak go to the wall.
Stephen	Did you stop them?
Hugh	No trouble.

A drunk shuffles in coughing.

Good morning, sir.

Man coughs.

This your first visit to our facility?

Man coughs again.

If you require our full relief service, the cubicles are to your left, otherwise you will find the quick service stalls situated ahead of you.

Man lurches away and vomits into a corner.

Dammit!

Stephen	Dammit, Peter, we're still not attracting the right kind of customer.
Hugh	I know, John. But a lot of the more desirable punters are going next door.
Stephen	And why in *hell* aren't they coming here?
Hugh	Because they're women, John.

Stephen	Peter, I want you to get in next door, and find out who's running their operation.
Hugh	I already know who's running it, John. It was quite a shock, I can tell you.
Stephen	Don't say it, Peter. Don't tell me ...
Hugh	That's right. Marjorie.
Both	DAAAAMN!

A Selected List of Humour Available from Mandarin

While every effort is made to keep prices low, it is sometimes necessary to increase prices at short notice. Mandarin Paperbacks reserves the right to show new retail prices on covers which may differ from those previously advertised in the text or elsewhere.

The prices shown below were correct at the time of going to press.

All these books are available at your bookshop or newsagent, or can be ordered direct from the publisher. Just tick the titles you want and fill in the form below.

Mandarin Paperbacks, Cash Sales Department, PO Box 11, Falmouth, Cornwall TR10 9EN.

Please send cheque or postal order, no currency, for purchase price quoted and allow the following for postage and packing:

UK   80p for the first book, 20p for each additional book ordered to a maximum charge of £2.00.

BFPO   80p for the first book, 20p for each additional book.

Overseas   £1.50 for the first book, £1.00 for the second and 30p for each additional book
including Eire   thereafter.

NAME (Block letters) ....

ADDRESS ....

....

....